T0128523

EVIDENCE *of*
GENUINE CONVERSION

EVIDENCE *of*
GENUINE CONVERSION

RICHARD W. BARTON

(FORWARD BY PHIL JOHNSON)

authorHOUSE®

AuthorHouse™
1663 Liberty Drive
Bloomington, IN 47403
www.authorhouse.com
Phone: 1-800-839-8640

Published by AuthorHouse   05/07/2012

ISBN: 978-1-4685-8876-7 (sc)
ISBN: 978-1-4685-8877-4 (e)

Library of Congress Control Number: 2012907143

Any people depicted in stock imagery provided by Thinkstock are models, and such images are being used for illustrative purposes only. Certain stock imagery © Thinkstock.

This book is printed on acid-free paper.

Because of the dynamic nature of the Internet, any web addresses or links contained in this book may have changed since publication and may no longer be valid. The views expressed in this work are solely those of the author and do not necessarily reflect the views of the publisher, and the publisher hereby disclaims any responsibility for them.

All Scripture is taken from the New King James Bible, unless otherwise noted.

All Scripture quotes in the main body of the text are in italics.

(Scripture taken from the New Kings James Version. Copyright © 1979, 1980, 1982 by Thomas Nelson, Inc. Used by permission. All rights reserved.)

CONTENTS

"Therefore brethren be . . . diligent to make your calling and election sure"
(2 Peter 1:10).

DEDICATION

This volume is dedicated to my father,
Richard W. Barton I, who at the
age of 96 put his faith and trust in the
Lord Jesus Christ and two years later
entered his eternal home.

FOREWORD

No careful reader of Scripture can possibly miss the fact that every major New Testament author, as well as Jesus Himself, frequently warned against the dangers of superficial and phony faith, false assurance, self-deception, and apathy about one's own spiritual condition. When the apostle Paul urged the Corinthians to, "Examine yourselves as to whether you are in the faith. Test yourselves" (2 Corinthians 13:5), he was summarizing one of the major themes of the New Testament.

Richard Barton became keenly aware of that strand of New Testament teaching several years ago and has devoted a significant amount of his life and energies to understanding what the Bible teaches about the difference between authentic saving faith and the superficial, half-hearted assent that Jesus warned could never save. Barton does an excellent job of making that distinction crystal-clear in language that is simple to understand and with biblical proofs that are impossible to dismiss.

A few years ago when the debate over "lordship salvation" dominated the evangelical agenda, I edited several well-known books dealing with the subject. (It was my privilege to edit both of John MacArthur's major books on the topic, *The Gospel According to Jesus* and *The Gospel According to the Apostles*). Those books were thorough and detailed, and would be excellent resources for further study by anyone whose interest is piqued by this book. But many readers encountering such a difficult and heated theological debate for the first time found the page counts of those books intimidating.

What was needed was a good, simple introduction to the subject. Several fine laymen's guides to the debate were written in the ensuing years, but none of them was as concise, simple, and easy to grasp as the work you are now holding in your hands. Richard Barton has given us a wonderful tool to use for those who need an introduction to the subject.

On an even more practical note, this is an excellent resource for believers who may be struggling with the validity of their own faith, or worse may be convinced their faith is genuine, but are self-deceived. My hope and prayer is that it will affirm the assurance of those who truly believe, while shattering the false confidence of any who are in bondage to a complacent self-deception, and be used of the Lord to enlighten many souls to the saving truth of the glorious gospel of Christ.

Phil Johnson
Executive Director of *Grace to You*
(Radio Ministry of John MacArthur)

Valencia, California
March 2006

PREFACE

Evidence of Genuine Conversion, though not a long book, is the product of tears, earnest prayer, the reading of good Christian books, and sitting under great expository preaching at Grace Community Church in Sun Valley, California where Dr. John MacArthur is our beloved Pastor and Teacher.

The actual genesis of this book began as a profoundly disturbing thought that not only troubled my soul but eventually settled into a conviction that there were those near and dear to me who *professed* Christ, but whose lifestyle indicated that they may not *possess* Him.

In the passing of time I became increasingly aware that *professing* Christ, without the *possession* of Christ, was widespread and epidemic in the Evangelical Church.

Countless people today claim faith in Christ, and say they are "*born again,*" yet for many of these same people, if their lives were placed beneath the searchlight of Scripture, there would be little or no resemblance to what the Bible calls, a "*new creation*" where "*old things have passed away*" and "*all things have become new*" (2 Corinthians 5:17).

Perhaps you are thinking to yourself, "This is not for me. I *know* that I am a Christian." Let me say that this book was not written to pass judgment on who is, or who is not, a Christian, but to present the *evidence* of salvation that Scripture gives. Heart examination concerning our eternal destiny is *not* optional. *All* Christians are *commanded* to, "*Examine yourselves as to whether you are in the faith*" (2 Corinthians 13:5). So if you are saying, "This doesn't concern me" you need instead to ask yourself, "Have I obeyed this command?" If not, then now is the time to do so. When you obey God's command your faith will be confirmed and strengthened, and for those who may be deceived this self-examination could alter your eternal destiny.

Let me conclude by asking you, "What could possibly be more important in life than making certain, beyond any shadow of a doubt, that heaven will be your home?" The Devil is active as an "*angel of light*" (2 Corinthians 11:14) in an effort to blind the minds of men and women to "*the light of the gospel of the glory of Christ*" (2 Corinthians 4:4). In these last days of the Church age Satan "*knows that he has only a short time*" (Revelation 12:12) and he is waging all out warfare against the one message that he knows can deliver the souls of men out of his hands. If he cannot prevent us from hearing the gospel he will do everything in his power to distort the message so that what men believe will be powerless to save them.

Salvation is the one subject above all others we must have clarity about, yet multitudes of people in the Church are deceived about their true spiritual condition. How can we so confidently say this? Because so many are basing their hope of heaven on *unbiblical* premises! What God says in His Word is *all* that matters! The burden of this book is to examine the evidences which the Word of God sets forth concerning who is, and who is not, a Christian. Our assurance of eternal life *must* be based on Scripture!

May it please God to use what has been written to open the eyes of any who may be deceived, and bring comfort and assurance to every true believer.

Richard W Barton

INTRODUCTION

"Examine yourselves as to whether you are in the faith. Prove yourselves." (2 Corinthians 13:5)

This scripture deals with the most important subject man's mind can be occupied with. Nothing in all of life even comes close to the importance of every person's conclusion regarding the above command by the Apostle Paul. Sadly, millions of earth's inhabitants, living under the deception of false religious beliefs, may never experience a true examination of their spiritual condition. To those of us who live in "Christian" lands and have full access to God's Word the command to *"examine yourselves"* is not only binding, but a cause for great thanksgiving.

The purpose of this book is to examine serious aberrant teaching in the church regarding who is and who is not a Christian, and to direct every honest seeker for assurance of salvation to the Scripture basis alone on which to base such assurance.

When the Apostle Paul spoke this command to the Church in Corinth he was not just speaking to the weak and the doubting among them. The Spirit of God directed this command to all believers. The pages of the Bible, especially the New Testament, contain various "proof texts" by which we can obey this command of God and accurately judge our own spiritual condition

Not only did Paul command this important spiritual exercise, but the Apostle Peter gave a similar command in his second epistle, "*Therefore, brethren, be all the more diligent to make certain about His calling and choosing you*" (2 Peter 1:10).

There is an alarming, long standing, trend within the Evangelical Church—one that has swelled church membership rolls with unnumbered people who are deceived about their true spiritual condition. Jesus said, "*Narrow is the gate and difficult is the way which leads to life, and there are few who find it*" (Matthew 7:14). If the Gallup polls are correct, and if the 88 percent of Americans who claim to be born again are truly born again, then Jesus was mistaken about the "*few*," but we know that, "*God, who cannot lie,*" (Titus 1:2) always speaks the truth.

This trend, of which we speak, is an easy believism that considers anyone a Christian if they have gone through certain "steps" in "receiving Christ," regardless of the kind of life they are living. These steps, so called, are widely used in public evangelistic endeavors. If this charge of "easy believism" is true, how is it that this trend developed? In actuality, the roots of this dilemma go back over 100 years.

"Deciding" For Christ

In bygone days the statement, "walking the sawdust trail" was a common euphemism of someone who had "gone forward" in a public evangelistic gospel tent meeting to make a "decision" for Christ. (The "sawdust trail" had reference to the sawdust that was scattered as ground covering inside the tent). While the phrase, "walking the sawdust trail" is not spoken of today, the evangelistic methodology used in connection with it remains pretty much unchanged. By way of definition, this methodology can be described as follows:

During evangelistic meetings, at the conclusion of a gospel message people were encouraged to "invite" Christ into their lives. They were asked to raise their hand if they wanted to "ask Christ into their heart." Those who raised their hands were invited to come forward, i.e. "walk the sawdust trail" to seal this decision. They would meet with a counselor, be asked various questions, and be invited to say a prayer to "receive Christ." In some meetings those who raised their hands were simply asked to repeat silently in their heart a prayer of receiving Christ right where they were seated. After praying the prayer of acceptance they were told that they were now born again.

While countless people have come to genuine saving faith in this way, there is a fatal flaw with such methodology. Nowhere in scripture do we find any of the above "steps" of evangelism as a *basis* for the *assurance* of salvation. (For that matter, no *experience* of any kind in scripture is ever considered to be a validation of saving faith). When Jesus was transfigured before Peter, James, and John scripture does not hold this "experience" up as the validation of their faith, but instead Peter, when speaking of this amazing experience, said, *"And we have something more sure, the prophetic Word, to which you will do well to pay attention,"* 2 Peter 1:19 ESV).

Scripture places the overwhelming weight for the evidence of our salvation in the *present* tense—on the kind of life we are *presently* living. We must *never* unequivocally assure someone of the certainty of their salvation just because they prayed a prayer to "receive Christ." It is the office of the Holy Spirit to give assurance, not ours. The only *valid* proof that anyone's prayer of receiving Christ was sealed in heaven is the resulting *change of life* that *always* follows genuine conversion! In spite of this plain teaching of Scripture there are multitudes of people, in the past and today, who have been told that if they have once "asked Christ into their hearts," they should *never* examine their salvation. This is contrary to the clear command of Scripture to, *"examine yourselves as to whether you are in the faith"* (2 Corinthians 13:5). Such erroneous and premature giving assurance of salvation only sets the stage for possible spiritual deception.

While the use of varying methods of evangelism is legitimate among evangelists, pastors, and lay persons we must always take great care to never alter the *content* of the Gospel message as outlined in Scripture, and thereby deviate doctrinally from *"the faith which was once for all delivered to the saints"* (Jude 3).

Before proceeding further, an important distinction needs to be made to avoid being misunderstood regarding the purpose and contents of this book. The distinction is this: God and God alone knows the hearts of all men, *"for man looks on the outward appearance but God looks on the heart"* (1 Samuel 16:7.) Nowhere in Scripture are we given license to pass ultimate judgment on a person's salvation. God alone sees into *"the heart,"* He alone knows with certainty its true condition.

Even though final judgment is Gods, various scriptures, and the Lord's own words, *"You will know them by their fruits,"* (Matthew 7:16) give to us authority to make an evaluation of a person's spiritual condition. This evaluation can only be based on the *"the outward appearance,"* which is the only evidence we have.

Please note, however, there is a world of difference between an "evaluation" judgment and an "ultimate" judgment. The ultimate judgment will be made by the Lord when stand before Him. We are fallible, God is infallible.

Having made this important distinction, the rest of this book then is basically an exposition of the biblical authority that we all have as believers to make an honest, scriptural, evaluation of not only someone else's spiritual condition, but also our own.

Is Sincerity Enough?

John MacArthur in his commentary on John's Gospel starts off his comments on John 3:1-10 (the encounter with Nicodemus) with these sad, but true, words:

> *"Everybody talkin' about heaven ain't goin' there." This line, from an old spiritual, accurately describes many in the church. Outwardly they identify with Christ, but inwardly they have never been genuinely converted. Because they cling to a false profession, they fool themselves into thinking they are on the narrow path leading to life, when in reality they are on the broad road that leads to destruction. To make matters worse, their self-deception is often reinforced by well-meaning but undiscerning Christians who naively embrace them as true believers. Such confusion stems from the watered-down pseudo-gospels that are propagated from far too many pulpits. Cheap grace, market-driven ministry, emotionalism, subjectivism, and an indiscriminate inclusivism have all infiltrated the church with devastating consequences. As a result, almost any profession of faith is affirmed as genuine—even from those*

> *whose lives manifest no signs of true fruit (e.g.,*
> *Luke 6:43-44). For many, no one's faith is to*
> *be questioned. Meanwhile key New Testament*
> *passages regarding the danger of false faith (e.g.,*
> *James 2:14-26) and the need for self-examination*
> *(e.g., 2 Cor. 13:5) go unheeded."* (Pages 97-98)

This is truly a concise, penetrating, assessment of the sad condition of much of the Evangelical Church of today. In our rush to be "relevant" (accepted) by an unsaved world we have taken a good motive (a desire to see people come to Christ) and have gone way beyond the bounds of orthodoxy, watering down the message in order not to offend anyone. The result is that multitudes are being deceived into thinking they are right with God because they have jumped through all the hoops we have set for them. The common practice is to put everyone under one big salvation umbrella with the only criteria being, "Did you pray the prayer?" Sincerity, we are told, is enough no matter what you believe! If you find that shocking, Paul McGuire, in his radio talk show on KKLA in Los Angeles, related that 68 percent of evangelicals believe that anyone will make it to heaven if they are good, and if they are sincere; regardless of their religious persuasion! This is an unbelievable statistic coming from those who profess to believe the Bible! Who needs Jesus? In actuality a statistic such as this simply highlights and exposes the sad condition of many in the Evangelical Church, revealing just how far down the road from sound doctrine we have traveled.

Such statistics are indicative of the leadership within the Church. Why are so many who claim to know Christ biblically illiterate? Instead of pastors preaching expository sermons, and opening up to their congregations what

God has to say in His Word, most use a Bible text as a springboard and ramble on from there sharing nice thoughts and their own commentary, but never exegeting the text. Such preaching does not exalt the Word of God, or the God of the Word. It has produced a generation of Bible illiterates. While weak preaching doesn't excuse the layman from studying Scripture for himself (as Christian's are commanded to do in 2 Timothy 2:15) it does set a low example, and has a direct bearing on the doctrinal drift, and the compromised message that is popular today.

The Lordship Controversy

This book was never intended as an essay on the "Lordship Controversy" issue within the Church, but I realized after I had finished writing it that it may well have been just that, because it is the "no-Lordship" teaching that is feeding and multiplying the problem this book was written to confront—the problem of easy believism and widespread deception concerning salvation.

For anyone not familiar with the above controversy among evangelicals, "Lordship Salvation" is the term certain evangelical theologians have tagged those within the evangelical church who still hold that Scripture clearly teaches that one cannot genuinely come to Christ as Savior without also coming to Him as Lord. No one is more responsible for this "Lordship Salvation" tag then Pastor and Author, John MacArthur. His landmark book, *The Gospel According to Jesus*, sparked a firestorm of controversy that is still with us today. Those who are advocates of a no Lordship salvation have picked an argument with God, not John MacArthur. We have no lesser authority for such a claim than the Apostle Paul, who under the inspiration of the Holy Spirit, laid down the biblical absolute for genuine, saving, faith: "*if you confess with your mouth Jesus as **Lord**, and believe in your heart that God raised Him from the dead, you will be saved*" (Romans 10:9 NASB, emphasis mine).

Paul says that God's requirement for salvation is twofold:

1. Confess Jesus as *Lord*.
2. *Believe* that God raised Him from the dead.

It is not without note, that confessing "*Jesus as Lord*" is the *first* requirement given by Paul. What does confessing "*Jesus as Lord*" mean?" We find that answer in the Greek definition of the word. The word "*Lord*" is the Greek word "kurios." Strong's Concordance gives this definition: "(supremacy); *supreme* in authority, i.e. *controller*, by implication Mr. (as a respectful title): God, Lord, Master, Sir."

We all can understand the implication of the above descriptive words. Coming to Christ for salvation is *first* to make Him Lord–the "supreme," "controller," "master" of one's life, and is always coupled with a heart belief in His death and resurrection to pay for our sin. This alone is the Biblical formula, and we dare not tamper with what God's Spirit has given to us. Genuine conversion embodies full commitment, total submission, and obedience to all the precepts and commands of God as revealed in the Scriptures. We are not talking here of a *pre*-salvation work in order *to be* saved. No, this is speaking of a heart willingness and commitment, in the experience of salvation, to embrace Christ as your Lord that is *synonymous* with believing on Him. Does this sound even remotely related to the no-lordship advocates who contend that all the gospel requires of men to be saved is to "accept Jesus" as Savior? Lordship, they say, though desirable, can be received later. While this may "tickle our ears" and sound good it is not what Scripture says!

In 2 Corinthians 5:17 we read, "*Therefore, if anyone is in Christ, he is a new creation; old things have passed away; behold all things have become new.*" This verse *alone* should end the no Lordship controversy. To argue that one can come to saving faith in Christ and yet not necessarily manifest a changed life is to deny the teaching of the Word of God. God's Word says that *every* person who is "*in Christ*" (born again) *is* (present tense) a "*new creation,*" and that "*old things have* (past tense) *passed away,*" and that "*all things have* (present tense) *become new*" I don't see any time lapse anywhere in this verse.

As soon as we affirm that Scripture teaches that *how we live* has a bearing on the reality of our profession of faith in Christ, the no-lordship theologians throw up their hands and cry, "You are proclaiming a works salvation!" Our emphatic answer to them is, "No, we are not!" Salvation is by grace through faith *alone,* apart from any human work, but genuine saving faith can only be proven genuine, to a watching world, says the Apostle James, by our works. "*But do you want to know, O foolish man, that faith without works is dead?*" (James 2:20). Anyone can claim to have faith, but only a *changed life* makes that claim valid!

Contrary to our popular methods of evangelism, Jesus never made it "easy" to become a follower of His. He made the conditions hard, impossible actually, to human flesh. He never sought superficial commitments, but made it very clear that those who desired to follow after Him must, "*sit down first and count the cost*" (see Luke 14:28). He is not looking for "fair weather," "armchair" disciples. Becoming a Christian will cost you everything—it could even cost your life someday. "*If anyone desires to come after Me, let him deny himself, and take up his cross, and follow Me*" (Matthew 16:24).

When we come to Christ we take Him for Who He is. Yes, He is the Savior to be sure, but His *full* name is: The *Lord* Jesus Christ. We must receive Him in the fullness of that name.

This erroneous teaching, which inserts a time interval between His becoming our Savior at conversion and His lordship over our lives is referred to in Pentecostal and Charismatic circles as the "second blessing," or "full surrender," or, in evangelical circles as the Keswick, "let go and let God" teaching, as if full salvation comes in stages, or steps! This is man-made religion totally foreign to Scripture! No-Lordship advocates need to take note that the Scriptures *always,* in the context of evangelism, presents Christ as both *Lord* and Savior–in *that* order! Arthur W. Pink, a classic Reformed theologian of the twentieth century, stated the case very well:

> "*Saving faith consists of the complete surrender of my whole being and life to the claims of God upon me . . . it is the unreserved acceptance of Christ as my absolute Lord, bowing to His will and receiving His yoke. "As ye have therefore received Christ Jesus the Lord, so walk ye in Him" (Colossians 2:6). Yes, mark it well that Christ is "received" as Lord. Oh, how far, far below the New Testament standard is this modern way of begging sinners to receive Christ as their own personal "Savior." If the reader will consult his concordance, he will find that in every passage where the two titles are*

> *found together it is always "Lord and Savior," and*
> *never vice versa."*[1]

If Pink's comment, which is fully supported by Scripture, was believed by all evangelicals there never would have been a Lordship Controversy, but the hearts of men at times seem willfully blinded. It might be asked, "What lies at the root of this erroneous teaching?" Our answer would be that much if not all of this blindness can be attributed, as was already mentioned, to biblical illiteracy. It is sad that we have to apply to brethren the words of Jesus, which were intended for His enemies, "*Well did Isaiah prophesy about you . . . 'in vain they worship Me, teaching as doctrines the commandments of men'*" (Matthew 15:7, 9).

It has truthfully been said, "If He is not Lord *of* all, He is not Lord *at* all." An easy believism is the devil's pathway to false assurance, not heaven.

This blessed truth of Christ's Lordship, rather than proclaiming a works salvation and taking away from the simple gospel of grace through faith alone, in actuality *adorns* the gospel message since the faith to receive Him as Lord is a work of God, for ". . . *no one can say that Jesus is Lord except by the Holy Spirit*" (2 Corinthians 12:3).

The Difficulty of Becoming a Christian

Salvation is a free gift from God that is it not easily acquired. This ought not to shock anyone. Contrary to the "easy believism" that is so prevalent today when Christ called individuals to follow Him it was always a call to a *total* and a *costly* commitment, "*Whoever desires to come after Me, let him deny himself, and take up his cross, and follow Me*" (Mark 8:34). Notice in this verse the words, *"deny," "cross"* and *"follow."* Salvation is indeed offered freely, but to provide salvation costs God His only Son, and Christ His life, and it will cost us our self-life as well. *"For whoever desires to save his life will lose it, but whoever loses his life for My sake will save it"* (Luke 9:23). (This is not, primarily, a reference to martyrdom, although that possibility is included in our commitment, but Jesus was referring to dying to self-life).

When the rich young ruler came to Jesus seeking eternal life he went away disappointed, because he wasn't willing to give up his "god" which was money. Men today have their "gods," but to follow Christ we must forsake our idols. (An idol is not only a statue that pagans bow down to, but is *anything* more important than God in our lives). Jesus calls all who would follow Him to a total surrender to Himself and to His Kingdom even if that should mean death. He said that the way to eternal life was *"narrow"* and *"difficult,"* and that *"few"* would find it. Sadly, He went on to say that *"many"* would be unwilling to come the narrow way, *"for wide is the gate and broad is the way that leads to destruction, and there are many who go in by it"* (Matthew 7:13).

If it is not easy to be saved, and if the majority of mankind will choose not to enter the *"narrow gate,"* then how can we know whether or not we are among the *"few"* Jesus spoke of? If the consequence of not believing, or of believing wrongly, is eternal hell then surely God would not leave us without some clear way of examining our hearts as to whether or not we belong to Him. The good news is He did not leave us to wonder, or to hope about this all important matter in life. He inspired the Apostle John to pen this comforting verse, *"These things have I written to you who believe in the name of the Son of God, that you may know that you have eternal life"* (1 John 5:13).

Before we get into chapter one where we will begin to exposit some of the scriptural evidences of genuine conversion that can assure us of a *"know"* so salvation the Apostle John spoke of, it will be helpful to look at what the Bible says transpires in the heart at the moment of conversion. If we correctly understand the miracle of the new birth, it will go a long way in understanding the matter of assurance.

A New Creation

In 2 Corinthians 5:17 we read, *"Therefore if any man be in Christ he is a new creation, old things have passed away, behold all things have become new."* At salvation we pass from a state of death into life, (John 5:24) and we become a *"new"* person.

The core truth about salvation is that genuine conversion brings about a brand new creation into our nature. Before conversion, no matter how refined or moral we might have been we were all slaves to the sin nature that was passed down to us from Adam. We were separated from God and spiritually dead, but when God in His sovereign grace reached down to rescue us, in that moment of conversion a true miracle takes place, and the living God, in the person of the Holy Spirit, takes up *permanent* residence in our hearts, and we become, *"partakers of the divine nature"* (2 Peter 1:4), a *"new man"* (Colossians 3:10). We suddenly find ourselves *loving* God, *desiring* His will, *hating* sin, and *wanting* to obey. Instead of being separated from God we are now joined to Him in an eternal and inseparable bond. (Romans 8:38, 39). This change in our nature is a miracle every bit as great and supernatural as the creation of the universe.

No amount of education or self-reformation can ever bring about this spiritual transformation. This miracle is prophesied in the Old Testament and experienced fully in the New. In Hebrews 8:10, and again in 10:16, the writer quotes Jeremiah 31:33 in speaking of the *"new heart"* that God would give to believing Israel, and also to *all* mankind, under the New Covenant, *"This is the covenant that I will make with them . . . I will put My laws into their hearts, and in their minds I will write them"* (Hebrews 10:16).

Before we experience God's redeeming grace, the law of God is *external* to us. It commands what we are unable to perform. We may acknowledge the righteousness of God's law; even try our best to obey it, but it is nonetheless external. Only in the hearts of those in whom the Holy Spirit lives is the law of God *resident*—as a life principle *within*. That is why the Apostle Paul writes in his Epistle to the Colossians, *"Christ in you the hope of glory."* (Colossians 1:2). We have absolutely no *"hope of glory"* (heaven) apart from the new birth in which Christ comes to live within us. *"Now if anyone does not have the Spirit of Christ, he is not His"* (Romans 8:9). God's Holy law, which was impossible for us to keep, Christ kept in our place, and when we are born again through believing the gospel God credits Christ's perfect life of righteousness to our account and declares us not guilty! That is grace!

Because of this "amazing grace" once we are saved *everything* in life is seen in a whole new dimension. Everything changes! The Psalmist expressed it this way, *"I have set the Lord always before me"* (Psalm 16:8). What a wonderful truth this is. Before He was not *"in all our thoughts,*" now He is "*always before*" us. This is the blessed experience of all the regenerate. The hymn writer has beautifully captured this miraculous change that occurs the moment we believe:

> "*Heaven above is softer blue,*
> *Earth around is sweeter green*
> *Something lives in every hue*
> *Christ-less eyes have never seen!*
>
> *Birds with gladder songs o'er flow,*
> *Flowers with deeper beauties shine,*
> *Since I know as now I know*
> *I am His and He is mine.*"

(Stanza two of, *I Am His And He Is Mine*—
Wade Robinson, 1838-1877)

This change that takes place at conversion totally transforms our lives, raising our spirits from the dead and making us alive unto God. If this miracle has truly taken place in our hearts then we not only become a "*new creation*" but our lives radically change as well. This "*new creation*" within *always* produces a *radical* change without.

A Radical Change

The new heart God gives us at salvation makes us new on the *inside,* and brings about a radical lifestyle change on the *outside.* If you profess salvation but "*all things*" are not literally becoming new in your life, inwardly and outwardly, then you have very good reason to question the validity of your salvation experience. Charles Haddon Spurgeon said,

"*The grace of God that does not change you is not the grace of God.*" That is a biblical statement for it is impossible for the grace of God to come into a heart and make no noticeable difference. This lifestyle change in a true believer is at the heart of what this book is about. True salvation will be *seen*, not just experienced.

The Apostle Paul said about the change in his life after his conversion, "*It is no longer I who live, but Christ lives in me; and the life which I now live in the flesh I live by faith in the Son of God Who loved me and gave Himself for me*" (Galatians 2:20). This is radical talk! The old Paul was gone. The new Paul lived a completely different life!

Born of the Spirit

In the familiar narrative of Jesus and Nicodemus, in the third chapter of the Gospel of John, Jesus, in verse eight, makes a simple, yet profound, statement in regards to the work of the Holy Spirit in regeneration, He said, "*The wind blows where it wishes, and you hear the sound of it, but cannot tell where it comes from and where it goes. So is everyone who is born of the Spirit*" (John 3:8). What was our Lord, in using this word picture, telling Nicodemus and us?

Jesus was saying that the actual experience of the new birth, when a lost person crosses that unseen line and passes "*from death unto life,*" (John 5:24) is a sovereign miracle that cannot be observed with the physical eye. Just as the wind is invisible, yet real, even so salvation, though not experienced visibly, is nonetheless real. We cannot see the wind but we know it is a real force because we can hear it, feel it, and see the *evidence* of its reality by the things it touches all around us. The same is true with everyone who is born of the Spirit. While the actual transaction of salvation is invisible the resulting *evidences* of salvation are not. Just as our ears hear the sound of the wind, and our eyes see it's working, so the work of the Spirit of God in a human heart will become manifest in outward *visible* ways. Paul said, *"all things . . . become new"* (2 Corinthians 5:17). Salvation *changes* everything!

At conversion God changes us inwardly, in a moment of time. The outward changes are progressive and lifelong. The internal changes happen first–love for God and His Word, the love, joy and peace that flood our souls over sins forgiven and guilt removed. As we feed upon the Word of God, converse with Him in prayer, and fellowship with other believers in a biblically sound church will we experience the progressive growth of sanctification in which old habits and old sinful patterns are replaced with new, holy, patterns. No two believers will have the same sanctification experience. For some, outward changes are almost immediate, for others, it is more gradual, but for *all* there *will* be changes. Without this ongoing, lifelong, transformation any claim to salvation is false. *"The path of the just is like the shining sun, that shines ever brighter unto the perfect day* (Proverbs 4:18). Embracing Christ as Lord in salvation is only the beginning of the sanctification process.

Jesus said to Nicodemus in John 3:3, *"Most assuredly I say to you unless one is born again he cannot see the kingdom of God."* The transformation that takes place at conversion is so radical and life changing that Jesus compared it to being "born again." Every human birth is a radical transition from one mode of existence to a new and different one. We leave the dark protected world of our mother's womb and enter into the bright and dangerous environment of the world outside. The new birth is no less radical.

As surely as our *sin* nature will, in time, manifest itself following our birth into this natural world, so will our *new* nature, in time, manifest itself following our birth into the spiritual world. The sin nature we all receive from Adam, in our first (natural) birth, cannot be hidden; it will *always* manifest itself in various *acts* of sin. In the same way, the new nature we receive from God, in our second, (spiritual) birth, cannot be hidden; it will *always* manifest itself in various *acts* of righteousness.

The late A.W. Tozer, often spoken of as, The Twentieth Century Prophet, who was greatly used of God in his day, and still is through his writings, said in relation to this change of heart and life as a result of genuine conversion:

> *"Plain horse sense ought to tell us that anything that makes no change in the man who professes it makes no difference to God either, and it is an easily discernible fact that for countless numbers of persons the change from no-faith to faith makes no actual difference in the life . . ."[2]*

In the same vein, Bishop J.C. Ryle, well known English churchman of the nineteenth century, had this to say about justification and consequent sanctification in his great work, *Holiness*:

> *"Justification is the act of God about us, and is not easily discerned by others. Sanctification is the work of God within us, and cannot be hid in its outward manifestation from the eyes of men".[3]*

This truth of a changed life that is seen by, "*the eyes of men*" is so very important, and yet it is a truth that is neglected and ignored by today's evangelical church. Because of the easy believism that is prevalent, as long as one claims to have "received Christ," or to have made a "decision" they are embraced as fellow-believers, regardless if they do or do not manifest a transformed life. The result of this unscriptural lack of emphasis on what God's Word clearly teaches about true conversion is that the church is filled with unsaved, "intellectual" believers, whose hearts have never been made alive in Christ, and whose unchanged patterns of living bear mute testimony to their unchanged hearts.

How do you know that you are a *possessor* of eternal life and not just a *professor*? Ask yourself the following, "Do I have a:

—deep and unchanging love for Christ?
—ongoing pursuit to know God's Word?
—desire to live a life of complete obedience?
—longing to be holy?

If we say that we have been born again, but our life does not evidence a "*new* creation," in the inward man and a "*radical* change," of the outward man where we have ceased living a self-centered life and have begun to live a God-centered, others-centered, life, then whatever our experience may have been it was not true conversion.

In light of all that has been said, and of God's commands to "*examine*" ourselves, and to "*prove*" ourselves, and to "*know*," and "*make certain*" of our salvation, just how are we to proceed in obeying the Lord?

The Bible contains various "tests" that we can use in this all important self-examination. The following six evidences, taken from Scripture, are not exhaustive but are presented with the earnest prayer that the Holy Spirit will use them to illuminate each mind and heart, giving each person a true understanding of their relationship to the living God.

CHAPTER ONE

God's Love in the Heart

The first evidence of genuine saving faith is:

1. A true believer *possesses God's love* in their heart.

> "*The love of God has been poured out in our hearts by the Holy Spirit who was given unto us*" (Romans 5:5).

The first and most important evidence of salvation is a supernatural love *from* God and *for* God that enters our hearts at the moment of conversion. The Bible says that the Holy Spirit is "*given unto us*" at salvation, and that when He comes to live within us, "*the love of God*" is "*poured out in our hearts.*" This is not a human level of love; it is God's supernatural, agape, love—the kind of love that is God's alone, a kind of love we could never know or experience apart from God's revealing it and giving it to us. This love is what God in His essence *is*—"*for God is love*" (1 John 4:8). The love God imparts to us when we believe on Him is a love that has two-dimensions—love *for* God, and love *from* God for mankind.

Before we look at these two dimensions it is important to say that the love given to us by God at salvation is not to be defined, primarily, as a feeling—e.g. the "warm fuzzies," or as the Mormons say, "a burning in the breast." Feelings in themselves are never a reliable guide concerning spiritual things. This is true because feelings are common to all men—Christian and non-Christian, and are subject to fluctuation. The followers of false religions feel deeply, and have emotional attachments to their false gods, and likewise multitudes who profess faith in Christ are deceived into believing they must be right with God because they become emotional over spiritual things. Tears may well up while listening to a baptismal testimony, or a powerful sermon, or a stirring piece of Christian music, but emotional experiences are never to be the indicator of our true spiritual condition. Thomas Boston in his profound Puritan Classic, *Human Nature in Its Fourfold State,* said concerning salvation and emotions: *"There may be a wonderful moving of the affections in souls that are not at all touched with regenerating grace. When there is no grace there may, notwithstanding, be a flood of tears, as in Esau, who 'found no place of repentance, though he sought it carefully with tears'" (Hebrews 12:17).*[4]

To equate feelings and emotional experiences with spirituality can open the door to doctrinal errors of all kinds. The modern-day Charismatic movement is a prime example of this fact. While God's love in our hearts certainly does, and will, affect our emotions, in scripture love is predominantly defined as action, not emotion, *"God so loved . . . that He gave His only begotten Son"* (John 3:16), *"If anyone loves Me he will keep My word"* (John 14:23), *"Love is patient, and is kind . . . does not behave rudely . . ."* (1 Corinthians 13:4). The above scriptures concerning love, expressed both positively and negatively, deal with what we *do* rather than how we *feel.* The real test of God's love in our hearts is not determined by emotional feelings or experiences, but by how we *live out* the profession of our faith. The Apostle John made clear what the result of God's love in our hearts ought to be, "*My little children let us not love in word or in tongue, but in deed and in truth.*" (1 John 3:18). The love of God in a believer's heart is made manifest through action, i.e. "*deeds.*"

Having defined what this love from God is, we will look at the first of the two dimensions of supernatural love that God imparts to us at salvation—love *for* God.

Love for God

No one, apart from the experience of a spiritual new birth can love God in the way He requires and deserves. As was pointed out in the Introduction, the transformations that are simultaneous with a genuine conversion experience are a *new creation* of our nature, and a *radical change* in our lifestyle. The immediate proof of salvation is a love for God that was not present before. This is indeed a miracle. No one is born with a love for God. The very opposite is the case: "*The wicked are estranged from the womb; they go astray as soon as they are born, speaking lies*" (Psalm 58:3). We are born rebels. We not only do not love God but are in active opposition to Him! The unsaved, for the most part, are blind to this truth and would protest that such is not the case with them, but, "*let God be true and every man a liar*" (Romans 3:4.) How does God view every man or woman prior to conversion? We don't have to search hard for the answer: "*When we were enemies we were reconciled to God through the death of His Son*" (Romans 5:10.) Without the new birth God considers us all His "*enemies!*"

Many, as expressed above, will find these things hard to accept, and may even be offended but this in no way alters what God has said in His Word regarding the nature of the human heart. We may have been brought up in the Church, believing and knowing all about God, and may even have made a profession of faith in Christ at some point in our lives, and still be unconverted and lacking a genuine love for God. It is all too possible to know God in the head only! This is the condition of countless numbers within the established Church. These "Christians" are persuaded of the *facts* of the gospel and do not doubt for a moment the essential doctrines of the Christian faith, i.e. the birth, death, burial and resurrection of Christ. These people believe He is the Son of God, that He died for their sins, and that He is the only Savior. In other words, they are orthodox, and yet they may be on the road to hell! How can this be? It is possible because head knowledge alone is insufficient for salvation. Matthew Henry, well-known Bible commentator of a bygone era, said, "*Strong convictions often come short of sound conversions.*" How true!

Genuine saving faith is always an affair of the heart! If our profession of faith hasn't first of all *changed* our heart and brought about a different way of living then whatever we may have it is not salvation! This is so patently true in Scripture and in the real life experience of saints down through the ages that Jonathan Edwards, that great theologian of the Great Awakening in America, wrote a *whole* book, 382 pages long, titled: *Religious Affections*, in which he made unarguably clear that when God's Spirit enters a heart He *changes* its *affections*; not just superficially, but essentially, and eternally!

The title of a powerful gospel tract reads: "*Missing Heaven by 18 inches.*" This 18 inch distance, it points out inside, is the distance between the head and the heart and consequently the distance between heaven and hell! How tragically true this is for untold numbers of people.

Multitudes believe the *facts* of the gospel who have never allowed those facts to make the 18 inch trip to their hearts. They acknowledge the facts but stop short of a full surrender and commitment of themselves to Christ as their Savior *and* as their Lord. Facts never saved anyone! You may not doubt that He is the Savior, but have you ever enthroned Him as Lord?

And here again, with the above statement, we are up against the Lordship Controversy issue. Jesus is not just our Savior, but our Savior *and* Lord. If He is not the Lord of your life then He just may not be your Savior either. Regeneration is a one time event and doesn't come in stages. The only way I can believe He is your Savior is by what I can see He has done in your life! Scripture is clear: "*If you confess with your mouth that Jesus is Lord, and believe in your heart that God raised Him from the dead you will be saved. For with the heart one believes and is justified, and with the mouth one confesses* (i.e. His Lordship) *and is saved*" (Romans 10:9, 10 NEB, addition mine). *Confessing* Jesus as Lord is mentioned first and is every much a part of the above verse as *believing* in your heart. They are the two sides of the salvation coin.

Genuine love for God, that results in a transformed life is the wellspring and fountain of all else in the Christian life. It is the chief of virtues which is why Scripture says it is the fulfilling of the whole law (Romans 13:10). This is why it is first in importance. It is this God-given love for God which enables us to obey the first and greatest commandment in the law, "*You shall love the Lord your God with all your heart, with all your soul, and with all your mind*" (Deuteronomy 6:5).

As love for God is first in importance it is consequently the first and greatest test of salvation. It is sure and certain proof of new life. Jesus taught there would be tares in the church that would be hard to distinguish from the real thing. There are many in the professing Church who appear, outwardly to men, to be true believers, but only those who know God (not just intellectually, but in their hearts) can truly love Him as the law commands. To love God like this is completely impossible to fallen man. John Piper, in his excellent book, *God's Passion for His Glory*, quotes Jonathan Edwards in regards to this miraculous change in our affections that takes place towards God at conversion:

> *"The first effect of the power of God in the heart in regeneration is to give the heart a Divine taste or sense; to cause it to have a relish of the loveliness and sweetness of the supreme excellency of the Divine nature."*[5]

What Jonathan Edwards was really saying in the above quote is, at conversion we, in essence, fall in love with God. We are drawn to who He really is in all His perfections. This "Divine taste or sense," these lofty thoughts of God are not experienced by the unconverted.

Before conversion every person's life is man centered, i.e. centered on self and the material world. It cannot be otherwise, because, *"No one knows the things of God except the Spirit of God. Now we have received, not the spirit of the world, but the Spirit Who is from God, that we might know the things that have been freely given to us by God . . . the natural man does not receive the things of the Spirit of God . . . nor can he know them, because they are spiritually discerned"* (1 Corinthians 2:11-14).

While many claim love for God and Christ, if that claim is rooted only in a head knowledge and mental ascent to the facts, their daily lives will not support that claim.

The way they live will not bear witness to what they profess to believe. This is not to say that everyone professing faith in Christ is living in gross sin, but if it were possible to get inside their minds (which God, of course, can) we would immediately see that their thought life does not habitually ascend up to God in loving communion and fellowship throughout the hours of each day. Behind closed doors we would also discover that they do not habitually nurture their souls in consistent, daily, searching of the Scriptures, in times of prayer, in the reading of good Christian books, and the offering up of thanksgiving and continual praise in their hearts. They will not be fully committed to the church in faithful attendance, or in Christian service. They will not regularly seek out opportunities to practice good works, they will not give proportionately of their income to the Lord's work, and they will not have a heartfelt burden to share the gospel with others. In short, they do not live the *whole* of their lives unto God.

What is it to be a Christian? If the gospel doesn't *change* us profoundly from the way we lived *before* our professed conversion then our professed "conversion" was merely an ascent to a set of facts which have not yet made the 18 inch trip to our hearts.

Sadly, for many, God is, in reality, only an addition to their already busy lives. He is clearly not the *center,* out of which all else derives purpose and meaning. This is not salvation but deception. Every born again child of God should be able to say, from the depths of his, or her, heart with the Apostle Paul, "*For to me, to live is Christ . . .*" (Philippians 1:21).

And lest someone reading this become discouraged, to quote Pastor John MacArthur, "*We are not talking here of the perfection of the life, but of the direction.*" Only Christ lived a perfect life of course. Perfection for us is unattainable in this life, but if the "direction" of our life is a longing to be as much like Christ as possible it is a good sign of true conversion.

Jesus gave us a "litmus test," so to speak, concerning genuine love for Him. He said this, *"He who has my commandments and keeps them, it is he who loves Me. If anyone loves Me, he will keep My word . . . He who does not love Me does not keep my words"* (John 14:21, 23, 25). This is plain talk. There is no mistaking what Jesus said, or what He meant. In the eyes of God, love and obedience are one and the same. Genuine love *for* God means obedience *to* Him. If there is no consistent obedience there is no true love regardless of what we say. If our personal (behind closed doors) lives, as well as our outward public lives, are not different from before our professed conversion, then our verbal expressions of love to Christ are meaningless. If you are saved you will delight in obeying Him, and God's priorities will become your priorities. If you are not keeping His commandments and living your life under His Lordship, then according to Scripture, you don't love Him, it's that simple. And if you don't love Him then how can you claim to really know Him? Blunt? Yes, but it is the Word of God.

So much more could be said, but any person, who is brave enough to be fully honest, knows better than anyone else the true condition of their heart. We all know what the *motivating* drive of our life really is, whether it is *God* and *His* glory, or whether it is *self* and *our* interests. And in case we have fooled our own selves in this regard, a simple examination of our priorities will usually supply us with an accurate indicator of the bent of our heart:

Self-Check Test

Ask yourself, "*Who,* and *what* really has first place in my heart?" What is the first item on your list when you get up in the morning? Is it time with the Lord, even if your personal schedule only allows you a very limited time? Or instead do you switch on the TV, or the radio, or read the newspaper, etc., etc., and God is put on the back burner, or not given a place at all? But some will say, "This all sounds like law not grace—are we not free in Christ? Is it fair to judge someone by these kinds of things?" My reply, in all love, (seeking to be sympathetic to demanding schedules and difficult circumstances) is that this very question in itself is revealing. Putting God first in all things (which requires discipline to be sure) is not a duty but a joy! Yes, we are free in Christ, but the heart that is truly free in Christ will *desire* to put Him first in all things, not out of a sense of duty but because we want to please Him. The question of who, or what, has first place in our lives should not even need to be asked, or even be an issue! A slave (a scriptural designation for every believer) lives to please his master, not himself.

Question: Are God's interests, or self-interests, the real priorities in your life? Is God "*in all your thoughts*" as you live the *whole* of your life unto Him? Is He the *center* around which all else revolves? Do you seek His face daily in His word and prayer—not out of duty, but out of love? Can you say that you love God? If so, does your professed love prove itself genuine by your desire for *obedience*—obedience which is seen in a holy life, in faithful, sacrificial, service, and by good works? Does the anticipation of someday hearing from His lips, "*well done good and faithful servant*"

(Matthew 5:21) motivate you to an increasingly greater love and obedience? All these things, and more, are daily realities in a heart in which the love of God dwells.

These things we are speaking about may bring the charge of legalism, but these are the things that reveal the true state of our hearts.

A heart, in which the Spirit of God has done a true work of grace, will agree with Matthew Henry, "*When the law of God is written in our hearts, our duty will be our delight.*"

Only the miracle of the new birth can bring about this kind of a transformation. Love to God, in the big and in the "little" things, has always been the experience of regenerated men and women down through the ages. David, "[the] *man after God's own heart*" voiced the heart inclination of all truly converted souls, "*Oh, how I love your law! It is my mediation all the day*" (Psalm 119:97).

Love for mankind

Following love for God, the second manifestation of God's love dwelling in our hearts is love for mankind. This love for others is expressed in love for fellow believers, and love for the lost.

Love for fellow believers

Next to love for God, a true believer will love all those who love God. Jesus said our love for one another, within the fellowship of His Church, would be an *identifying mark* of being His disciple, "*By this shall all men know that you are my disciples if you have love one for another*" (John 13:35).

While we are to love all men, the Lord is speaking specifically in the above scripture of our love for fellow believers. He says that the world at large will bear witness that we are followers of Christ by our love for our brothers and sisters in the Church. One cannot profess to be a follower of Christ and remain apart from the life of the Church. The New Testament knows of no such Christian. We are *commanded* by God to, *"not [forsake] the assembling of ourselves together,"* and *"through love* [to] *serve one another"* (Hebrews 10:25, Galatians 5:13). Our love, says the Apostle John, is not to be *"in word or in tongue"* but in *"deed and truth"* (1 John 3:18). In other words, talking about loving others is one thing, but it is only the *demonstration* of love that authenticates our words. How can we say the love of God is dwelling in our hearts if we demonstrate no real love for God's people; or show no desire to serve God through serving His people? If we are not vitally connected with a body of believers, united in common worship, using our spiritual gifts in faithful ministry, it is indicative of one of two things: either we are disobedient, or we are not saved.

Question: In what way do you love the Church—the body of Christ? Is your love in *"word and tongue"* only, or in *"deed and truth?"* What deeds can you point to? Are you using your spiritual gifts to serve in some way? Do you give of your income joyfully, and generously, out of what God has given to you so that God's kingdom on earth can advance? Do you love to talk with other believers about the things of God? Do you look forward to Sunday services, and being with God's people? Are Sundays, and other times of fellowship with believers, times of growth and blessing in your life? If God's love is dwelling in your heart you will answer yes to all of these questions.

(It is sad to note that many of today's evangelical churches have dropped the evening service. Why, we might ask? Could it be that the worship of God, on *His* day, is no longer a priority with us? Could it be that we have lost our first love? Are we so unthankful for God's abundant blessings, and is God so marginal in our lives that we cannot even devote *one* complete day out of seven to Him? If your church still has an evening service, do you attend? Some again will say this is splitting hairs, and being legalistic, yet I fear these kinds of questions are sadly symptomatic of the state of our hearts, and the fervency of our love for Christ.

Love for the lost

The third and final outworking of God's love in a believer's heart is a love for the lost. A true child of God not only loves God and other believers but loves *all* men. "*And may the Lord make you increase and excel and overflow in love for one another and for all people, just as we also do for you*" (1 *Thess. 3:12, Amp. Bible*).

The second greatest commandment in the law requires us to "*love your neighbor as yourself*" (Leviticus 19:18) Jesus went even further and said, ". . . *love your enemies*" (Luke 6:35).

We are by nature self-centered, but through the new birth we become "*partakers of the divine nature*" (2 Peter 1:4) and since "*God is love*" (1 John 4:8) He reaches out in love to all men (cf. John 3:16, Romans 5:8) and we too, because He lives in us, will love all people, "*because as He is so are we in this world*" (1 John 4:17).

All Christians are commanded by Christ to bring the gospel to the lost (Mark 16:15). A burden for souls is not only obedience to the great commission, but is Godlike, and evidence that we ourselves have experienced His saving grace in our hearts.

The Apostle Paul said, in regards to sharing the gospel, "*the love of Christ constrains us*" (2 Corinthians 5:14). He is saying that the love of Christ for lost mankind moves and compels us to share the gospel. If that burden is not yours something is wrong. Charles Haddon Spurgeon in his book, *Being God's Friends,* had this to say about 2 Corinthians 5:14:

> "*We often hear people quote that passage as, 'The love of Christ ought to constrain us,' but that is a corruption of the text. The Apostle tells us that the love of Christ does constrain us. And if it really enters the heart it will do so. It is an active, moving power, influencing the inner life and then the external conduct.*"[6]

Knowing Christ and sharing Christ are inseparable. If we know Him we *will* experience His burden for the lost, and that burden will motivate us to action.

Being used of God to bring another person to a saving knowledge of Christ is one of life's most wonderful joys. There is nothing greater we can do for another human being then to introduce them to the only Person who can forgive their sin, take away their guilt, and change their eternal destiny! No true believer can rest content with a life that is not sharing Christ with others. Not all Christians are called by God to be Evangelists, but *all* are called to evangelize! Some people are by nature bolder and less inhibited than others, but we must overcome our timidity in obedience to Christ and out of compassion for the lost. Eternal souls hang in the balance! May we never forget that one of the most blessed facts about heaven is also one of the most horrifying facts about hell—both are eternal!

If you claim to be a true believer, and yet have little, or no, burden for the lost, then you are a disobedient Christian or maybe not a Christian at all. If you are a believer and find this to be true of you then you need to repent, put aside your fears, and ask God to give you courage and the right words to share the gospel. *Make* time to learn *how* to share the gospel and then *obey*! We do not have to be expert theologians to share the Good News. Sharing Christ is essentially being a witness to what He has done in your life. We don't lack the ability to witness; we lack obedience to act on our ability. Peter assures us that God has given us: "*everything that pertains to life and godliness*" (2 Peter 1:3) and this includes the power to witness.

Let it be said too, that, having a burden for souls does not mean that we are to be under a self-generated compulsion to share the gospel with everyone who crosses our path. The Holy Spirit, if we are sensitive to His leading, will bring us divine appointments. Sharing Christ in *His* power, and in *His* timing, is a successful witness, regardless if it brings that person to a decision. We just need to be sensitive to those we meet on a daily basis, and we must not be ashamed of the gospel. We should look on every encounter as a Divine encounter but we do not want to force doors open, but enter the ones the Spirit opens. Remember too, face-to-face sharing of the gospel isn't the only way of reaching the lost. It needs to be a major part of our witness, but tracts, letters, giving, praying, etc., are also legitimate and effective means of sharing Christ with a lost world.

Our love for others, in summary, is first and foremost a love for their spiritual welfare—for believers to edification, and for unbelievers for their salvation, yet, because God *is* love, a true believer, who is a partaker of God's nature, will live a *life* of love in our contacts with others, apart even from purely evangelistic motives. We are to, "*Walk in love, as Christ also has loved us, and given Himself for us*" (Ephesians 5:2.).

The character of love is self-sacrifice. A true evidence of conversion is a love that is manifested by us in the daily course of living our lives,—kindness, patience, gentleness, words of comfort and cheer, concern for the poor, various good deeds, and giving of our time and energy to both Christians and non-Christians.

If we are sharp, harsh, and unkind in our words, and show little of a "*gentle and quiet spirit, which is in the sight of God of great price*" (1 Peter 3:4), if we don't seek to serve others, and be a blessing wherever we may go, then we do not have the love of God dwelling in us. Love (*demonstrated love—love in *action*) is *true* Christian living, and is a witness to others that God has done a transforming work of grace in our hearts

Question: Do you have a love for the lost? Do you manifest a burden for the eternal souls of the men and women, and boys and girls all around you? Are there names of people, right now, on your heart for whom you are concerned? Are you seeking to share Christ with them? Does your heart ache at the thought of loved ones, friends, neighbors, and even your enemies spending an eternity in hell? Do your tears ever flow over their hopeless plight? Does the awful realization of eternal punishment move your heart to warn them? Do you fervently pray for the unsaved in your family, and outside it? Do you invite them to church? Do you make use of gospel tracts, write letters, visit, and give of your finances to reach them?" Are you in involved in Missions?

Are you walking in love before all men? Are you a blessing, or a source of friction? Jesus said, "*Follow Me and I will make you fishers of men*" (Matthew 4:19). Notice what Jesus says will happen to those who follow Him, "*I will make you fishers of men.*" If you are not "*fishing for men,*" then, how can you say you are a follower of Jesus? If the above activities and heart attitudes are not characteristic of your life, then you need to ask yourself, "Am I a true believer?"

CHAPTER TWO

Obedience

The second evidence of saving faith is:

2. A true believer *lives* an *obedient* life.

> "*Whoever keeps His word, truly the love of God is perfected in him. By this we know that we are in Him*" (1 John 2:5).

We have touched upon the importance of obedience in chapter one, now we want to look in depth at obedience as an evidence of salvation.

In the above scripture the Apostle John speaks very plainly about how we can know we have genuine faith, a faith that assures us "*that we are in Him.*" What is it that gives us this solid assurance? The Apostle answers in just four words, "*Whoever keeps His word.*" There is nothing difficult about knowing if you are one of God's children—God's children are *obedient*! It logically follows that those who don't belong to God are not obedient! True biblical faith *always* produces a life of obedience. When you have someone claiming a relationship with Christ but living a disobedient life there are only two possibilities: they are unsaved, or saved and disobedient.

This second evidence of saving faith is crucial, and is by and large missing in the "no Lordship" mentality of the Evangelical Church of today where anyone and everyone is considered "within the fold" if they have followed the right procedure, and said the right prayer. In the Bible faith and obedience are *synonymous* terms in describing a true believer. Faith that proves genuine is not just a faith that believes the *facts* of the gospel, but a faith that is obedient to the facts! Lordship advocates say, "This is a works salvation!" We answer, not so! In the statement above the words, "proves genuine" are key. Scripture is very clear to make this distinction concerning faith and obedience. Obedience always *follows* faith, never *precedes* it. Faith in Christ always comes first, but once saving faith in Christ is exercised, the only way our faith is *proven* genuine is by the obedience that accompanies faith.

We do not teach a person has to obey the gospel before they can truly believe, that would be a heretical perversion of the gospel. But to say, as the no Lordship advocates say, that obedience does not even enter into true saving faith is clearly a perversion.

The cry of the Reformation: "*The just shall live by faith*" championed by Martin Luther, is only one side of the gospel coin. The other side was succinctly stated by fellow reformer, John Calvin, who said, "Faith *alone* justifies, but the faith that justifies is *never* alone." (Emphasis added). What a great statement! What a powerfull condensation of what the Word of God teaches from start to finish! Calvin is not contradicting Luther, but only proclaiming what Scripture plainly teaches, that, "*faith without works is dead*" (James 2:20).

The Apostle Paul's words in the book of Romans, that the Holy Spirit used to produce saving faith in the heart of Martin Luther, and the Apostle James's words on the relationship of faith and works, are not conflicting doctrines. Salvation is by faith in Christ *alone*, apart from works, as Paul wrote, but from man's limited and fallible vantage point (since men cannot see into the heart) salvation can only be *verified before men* as genuine by the works that accompany it, as the Holy Spirit inspired James to write.

In the epistle to the Hebrews we read concerning the life of Jesus Christ that, "*though He was a Son, yet He learned obedience by the things which He suffered. And having been perfected, He became the author of eternal salvation to all who obey Him*" (Hebrews 5:9). Notice, what the inspired writer has said, Christ is, "*the author of eternal salvation to all who obey Him.*" Faith and obedience are so intimately intertwined in Scripture that anyone not familiar with the whole of Scripture might conclude from Hebrews 5:9 that God grants salvation *only* to those who *obey* Him, as if obedience is a *requirement* for salvation. Rather than teach a works salvation, this verse is a marvelous, and powerful, illustration, as we have been pointing out, of the *inseparableness* of faith and obedience.

What this verse *is* teaching is that salvation is *characterized* by obedience. Obedience is the sign and seal that the faith that we possess is genuine and saving.

(Having labored to say all that, there is one sense in which obedience *does* precede salvation, and it is this: We must *first* obey the command to repent before we can believe and be saved. The gospel Jesus preached was, "*Repent and believe in the gospel!*" (Mark 1:15). Yet even here, so there will be no grounds for boasting in God's presence, God *gives* to us the capacity to obey His command to repent, "*The goodness of God leads you to repentance*" (Romans 2:4).

19

"*Then God has also granted to the gentiles repentance to life*" (Acts 11:18).

The Son of God, (who was perfect and without sin) took on true humanity, and "*learned obedience*" (Hebrews 5:8) as an *example* and *pattern* for all future recipients of salvation who would "*follow His steps*" (1 Peter 2:21). As Jesus was obedient, we likewise are obedient. The saved, in Hebrews 5:9, are called, the "*all who obey Him.*" Obedience *defines* us as believers.

German pastor and author Dietrich Bonhaeffer, who suffered imprisonment under Adolf Hitler, once said, "*Only he who believes is obedient; only he who is obedient believes.*" This is not double talk, but gospel truth! It is only the saved ("*he who believes*") that are able to render the obedience that God requires, and it is only the "*obedient*" who give proof that they truly believe! (Bonhaeffer did not write out of theory, but out of real life experience; having paid with his life as a martyr for Jesus Christ near the close of World War II.)

Scripture then, as we have seen so far, identifies Christians as those who obey God, and it identifies non-Christians as those who do not obey God. The Apostle Peter, in contrasting the lost and the saved, says in 1 Peter 4:17, "*For the time has come for judgment to begin at the house of God; and if it begins with us first, what will be the end of those who do not obey the gospel of God?*" Peter could have said what he said here in a number of ways. He could have said, "What will be the end of those who have not believed on Jesus Christ?" Or, "What will be the end of those who have rejected the gospel, etc., etc.?" Instead he chose to designate the unsaved as "*those who do not obey the gospel of God.*" This is significant. God always says what He means and means what He says! We obey the gospel first by believing it, and we manifest that we *have* believed it by *continuing* to obey it! Peter is simply illustrating who the unsaved are, they are the ones who do *not* obey the gospel! Salvation and obedience in Scripture are *never* divorced.

The fallen human mind is skilled at self-deception. It is all too easy for us to fool ourselves. Those who are deceived about their salvation are often under the delusion that they *are* living in obedience. Because of this human tendency to deceive our own selves, we need to ask, "What defines the obedience of true saving faith? "What did Christ mean when He said that those who love Him would *obey* Him?" How can we know if we are living in obedience, and are not simply deceiving ourselves? As in everything in the Christian life it is not our opinion that matters, but what does God's Word have to say?

For the true believer obedience is not a list of do's and don'ts but an inward desire that springs out of a transformed heart—a new heart that delights in obedience, even in the unseen things that only God knows about. As I have stated earlier, it is possible to believe all the right things and still be lost. The difference is the indwelling Christ Who totally changes our sin nature and produces in us holy aspirations and longings.

The Importance of a Heart Change

A key phrase having to do with obedience is an "*inward desire*." This is the answer to our question, "How can we know if we are living in obedience and are not deceived?" A true believer has a *inward* heart *desire* to do God's will, and *delights* in it. An unbeliever does not—no matter how religious, or how well instructed in sound doctrine he, or she, might be. For the unbeliever, at the core of his, or her, being, obedience is the performance of a religious duty. That duty may often bring good feelings and make them happy.

Happiness and good feelings for the believer is simply a by-product; at the core of their being, obedience is a sacrifice of love which flows from a heart of thankfulness and grateful praise for salvation. Yet, because believers also are still in the flesh, obedience involves discipline, and at times we do grow weary, but nevertheless it is a willing and joyful discipline, never a religious duty. A true believer *longs* to live a life that is pleasing to God. In the inner man, the new man, we *delight* in obeying God as the Apostle Paul so clearly stated in Romans 7:22, "*For I joyfully concur with the law of God in the inner man.*"(NASB). Obedience, for the Christian, is positive, not negative. It is not trying to *avoid* doing wrong, but *delighting* in doing good. "*I delight to do thy will oh my God . . . Your law is within my heart*" (Psalm 40:8). This inward delight is another indicator of a genuine conversion experience.

In contrast, for unbelievers obedience is *doing* certain things, and *not doing* certain things. For example, if you ask an unbeliever if he, or she, is going to heaven a common answer is, "I hope so." If you probe further, and ask why God should let them into heaven, they will say something like, "Well, I have lived a good life," or, "I haven't murdered anybody," or, "I never committed adultery," or, "I don't cheat or steal," etc. etc. This is the standard reply from an unbeliever. They do not understand that true obedience to God is not *avoiding* certain *bad* things, and *doing* certain *good* things. God doesn't have a good and bad ledger in heaven by which He adds up the score, and in the end determines by this who He allows in.

I would like to point out here that there are different levels of unbelievers just as there are different levels of believers. Not all believers are at the same level of spiritual maturity, and not all unbelievers are at the same place in their spiritual understanding either. There are unbelievers who have little or no Bible knowledge, no church background, who still feel that (if there is a God) they are okay before Him. They believe that God has some type of scale or balance system in heaven by which He will weigh their good deeds against their bad deeds. Then there are unbelievers who are churched but who belong to a liberal denomination that has long since departed from sound doctrine. These individuals may attend church regularly, be active in social good deeds, read their Bibles, pray, etc., but have never seen themselves as lost sinners. They too feel they will make it to heaven. After all, they believe in God, go to church, do good deeds, etc. Then there is a class of unbelievers within the Evangelical fold—whose spiritual condition is the primary motive for writing this book. These are the "*tares among the wheat.*" They may have been taught from their youth the true gospel. They may have made a "decision" for Christ at some point in their lives, and may be active within their church. Concerning these, in His parable of the wheat and the tares, the Lord said not to pull up the tares because in so doing the good seed might be uprooted as well; so similar are they in appearance to the wheat. (Cf Matthew 13:24-30)

If Jesus said the Church would have tares in it, how is it that we are to distinguish the tares from the wheat? Tares, agriculturally, are very difficult to distinguish from wheat because they look so much like wheat. The key is in the harvest. Tares are worthless for food, they bear no real fruit. This is exactly how it is in the spiritual realm.

Professors in the true Church who have never allowed their head knowledge to become heart knowledge are very similar (outwardly) to true believers. They "know the language." This is not to say they are knowingly hypocritical, but they bear no *real* and *lasting* fruit. That is why Jesus said of His Church, "*By their fruits you will know them*" (Matthew 7:20). Tares in the spiritual realm profess repentance just as true believers do but they will lack the *genuine* fruit that *always* accompanies true repentance. We need to remember that God's estimation of the good deeds of the merely religious is that they are "*filthy rags*" (Isaiah 64:6) Paul's message to both Jew and Gentile in the book of Acts, and for us today, is, "*that they should repent, turn to God, and do works befitting repentance*" (Acts 26:20).

These "*tares among the wheat,*" that Jesus spoke of, may become offended if anyone expresses concern about their spiritual walk. This in itself may be an indication of their deception. All who truly know the Lord ought to be grateful for another brother or sister who cares enough about their souls to confront them in the spirit of Galatians 6:1.

The reality, and the evidence, of a true heart change that produces obedience is perhaps nowhere more graphically illustrated than in the Judgment of the Nations, in the Olivet Discourse, in Matthew 25:31-46.

Christ's Assessment of His True Sheep

Just prior to establishing His thousand-year reign on earth Christ assembles the nations before Him, and separates them, putting the sheep (the saved) on His right hand, and the goats (the unsaved) on His left. He first blesses the saved and invites them into His eternal kingdom, listing all the good works they did for Him by ministering to others. He then turns to the lost on His left and pronounces them to be cursed, listing the same good works they ought to have done for Him but failed to do by *not* ministering to others, and sends them away into the punishment of eternal fire.

It won't matter on Judgment Day what men "*professed*" to believe, but how they *lived out* what they professed to believe! Our deeds will either *support* our claim of faith or *deny* our claim. The words of Christ will condemn them, "*By their fruits you will know them*" (Matthew 7:20). It is quite easy to deceive men, but we can never deceive God. He sees all our deeds, or lack of deeds, but more importantly He sees the true motive of our hearts behind our deeds. "*There is no creature hidden from His sight, but all things are naked and open to the eyes of Him to Whom we must give account*" (Hebrews 4:13).

When we stand before God His judgment will be completely just. For unnumbered multitudes it will be their *lack* of good works that will be the telling proof of their true heart condition, but for multitudes more within the pale of Christendom (both liberal and evangelical) even the good works they will have done will not be the evidence of their salvation. This sad fact is revealed by Christ in Matthew 7:21-23. In verse 22 Jesus says that on the Day of Judgment there will be those, who professed on earth to know Him, who will say to Him, "*Lord, Lord, have we not prophesied in your name, cast out demons in your name, and in your name done many wonderful works?*" Imagine, here are people who have "*done many wonderful works*" in the name of Jesus! Surely these must be His children? But shockingly, Jesus will say to them, "*I never knew you, depart from Me, you who practice lawlessness*" (v 23). How can this be? This passage of Scripture tragically reveals that it is possible to identify with the Church, believe sincerely in Christ, think yourself to be a Christian, even *do* many good works in His name, and still be unsaved! How important then it is to examine our hearts! Only those whose *hearts* have been regenerated (not intellectual assent or doctrinal correctness) will hear Christ's "*well done*" on that day.

Non-believers can, and do, perform good works, but they are not good works prompted by the Holy Spirit, but are instead works of the human spirit. All that is good in this world goes back to God as its source. Human goodness finds its roots in that original image of God in which we were created. Human generated good works are commendable and beneficial, but they in no way earn nor verify a genuine relationship with God. An unsaved person may receive genuine pleasure from doing good works, and may even believe God is pleased with them, but God can never accept the good deeds of the unregenerate as having spiritual merit.

The works of the unconverted fall into the class of "social do-goodism," a phrase coined by pastor and author, John Piper. Only the works that arise out of a regenerated heart are acceptable to God. This is hard for sinful man to accept, but God says, "*We are all like an unclean thing, and all our righteousnesses are like filthy rags*" (Isaiah 64:6,). And in Psalm 14:2,3 we read, "*The Lord looked down from heaven upon the children of men to see if there were any who understand, who seek God. They have all turned aside, they have together become corrupt; there is none who does good, no not one!*" It is important to understand that even good deeds, which are certainly better than evil deeds, are not conclusive evidence of saving faith. As I said before, "All who are truly children of God *will* do good works, but not all who claim good works *are* truly children of God."

Millions from Pentecost on have claimed to be Christian who have never been born again. Multitudes are willing to embrace the teachings of Christ who are unwilling to make a heart commitment to His lordship over their lives. It is one thing to say you believe in Christ, even do good works in His name, but it is quite another thing to make Him *Lord* and *Master* of your life.

I have written extensively on the importance of the inner heart condition because of its incalculable importance in the matter of true saving faith, and consequently the obedience that springs from true saving faith. Solomon knew this by intimate experience when he penned these immortal words, "*Keep your heart with all diligence, for out of it are the issues of life*" (Proverbs 4:23.)

Jonathan Edwards felt the heart was of such great importance that he wrote an *entire* book titled: *Holy Affections*. In these two words he capsulized what takes place in regeneration. No unsaved person, no matter how orthodox they might be, ever has "holy affections." Holy affections are only born of the Spirit in a recreated heart

In concluding this chapter on obedience, I would ask, "What are the signs that one has these "holy affections" that Edwards wrote about? Each heart knows the answer to this question. We all know our own heart when it comes to its affections, allegiances and priorities. If you desire to know the true state of your heart I invite you to pray with David, "*Search me oh God and know my heart, try me and know my thoughts and see if there be any wicked way in me and lead me in the way everlasting*" (Psalm 139: 23, 24

No one else knows your heart but you and God. Ask yourself, "What is the true *inclination* of my heart in all areas of my life? Is Christ *Lord of all* to me? Can I say with the Apostle Paul, "*For to me to live is Christ*" (Philippians

1:21.) Do I value anything *above* Him? You may quickly say no, but would you still say no if all things in this life were taken from you? This has been the experience of countless saints down through the ages, men and women who forsook all and poured out their lives unto death to have Christ, and to be found faithful. These questions call for deep down soul searching. Ask God to grant you the grace to honestly examine your own heart. Ask Him for the searchlight of the Holy Spirit to look within to see if those holy affections are resident there. Holy affections are not something we work up by any effort of our own, but are a gift of God at salvation when we became *"partakers of the Divine nature"* and" *the love of God* [is] *shed abroad in our hearts"* (2 Peter 1:4, Romans 5:5.) *Then will I give them a heart to know Me, that I am the Lord"* (Jeremiah 24:7

Question: Look at your life, "Are you an obedient Christian? Jesus said, *"Why do you call Me 'Lord, Lord,' and do not do the things which I say?"* (Luke 6:46). Just what kind of Christianity is yours? Is it the armchair variety, or the soldier variety? Are you saying, *"Lord, Lord"* but doing little for the kingdom of God? Or is what you are doing simply because of your human affection for Christ rather than from a God given "holy affection?" Have the facts of the gospel, which you claim to believe, ever traveled the distance from your head to your heart? If all these things seem foreign to you then perhaps you need to rethink the validity of your conversion experience.

CHAPTER THREE

Fruitfulness

The third evidence of saving faith is:

3. A true believer *bears* spiritual *fruit.*

> "*By this my Father is gloried, that you bear much fruit and so prove to be my disciples*" (John 15:8, ESV).

In the second evidence of saving faith, concerning obedience, much was said about good works and its relation to obedience. In chapter three we want to look more fully at the subject of good works and/or spiritual *fruit* as a third evidence of genuine conversion.

A true Christian bears spiritual fruit The New Testament often uses the words "fruit" and "good works" in relation to our Christian life. What does the Bible mean when it speaks of a believer's fruit and/or good works? Is there a difference between them?"

Fruit and Good Works

The word "fruit," when used in connection with believers in the New Testament carries two basic meanings. First, the word fruit is used to describe *inward* virtue that is wrought in the heart by the Holy Spirit. "*The fruit of the Spirit is love, joy, peace, longsuffering, kindness, goodness, faithfulness, gentleness, self-control*" (Galatians 5:22). Secondly, the word fruit, is used to describe the *outward* good works a believer does in serving Christ—"*That you may have a walk worthy of the Lord, fully pleasing Him, being fruitful in every good work*" (Colossians 1:10) (As you can see from this verse in Colossians, sometimes the words "fruit" and "good works" are used interchangeably).

We will look first at the use of the word fruit as an *inward* virtue:

Inward Virtue

In Galatians 5:22 the Apostle Paul lists the nine-fold fruit of the Spirit, quoted above. This list of fruits (virtues) is, in reality, a description of the nature of God who indwells every believer. Since in regeneration we become "*partakers of the Divine nature*" these fruits are also resident in our new nature. Because mankind was created in God's image, unbelievers do show some reflection of God's nature even though the fall terribly distorted that image. But it is only in the life of a Christian that these attributes of God can develop into their fullest manifestation. These are not human produced fruits, but the supernatural fruit of the indwelling Spirit. 2 Corinthians 3:18 is the experience of the believer, "*But we all . . . beholding as in a mirror the glory of the Lord, are being transformed into the same image.*" Notice that the Holy Spirit says, "*all.*" If we claim salvation but our lives do not progressively reflect this ongoing transformation then our claim is empty.

Question: Has there been, and is there now, a continuing transformation in your life? Is it obvious to a lost world that something is different about you, about the way you live and relate to others? Can fellow Christians see a reflection of the likeness of Christ in you? While we all fall short of Christ-likeness, can you, as well as others, see this growth in the inward fruits of the Spirit? Are you growing in *love, joy, peace, patience, kindness, goodness, faithfulness, gentleness and self-control?* The Apostle James says to "*count it all joy when you fall into various trials*" (James 1:2). Are you able to find joy in your trials, because you know God is sovereign and good in all He does and allows? Have you experienced the Holy Spirit's power to walk in love, even when others treat you unfairly, or unkindly? Do you forgive others, or do you harbor a grudge? Are you seeking to grow in "kindness", "goodness" and "patience?" Do you practice "self-control" in your life? Unsaved people do not know this kind of living. When faced with trials they can only "grin and bear it," so to speak, with greater or lesser success, but it will only be the fleshly success of "mind over matter." Only the indwelling Holy Spirit can produce God-like virtue in us. The "*flesh*," Jesus said, "*profits nothing*" (John 6:63).

We go now to the second usage of the word fruit as descriptive of *outward* good works:

Outward Good Works

In Galatians 5:6 we read, "*For in Christ Jesus neither circumcision nor uncircumcision avails anything, but faith working through love.*" John MacArthur, author, radio speaker, and pastor of Grace Community Church in

Southern California, had this to say in commenting on this verse in *The MacArthur Study Bible,*

> *"Saving faith proves its genuine character by works of love. The one who lives by faith is internally motivated by love for God and Christ which supernaturally issues forth in reverent worship, genuine obedience, and self-sacrificing love for others."[7]*

This is a wonderfully definitive statement, and really covers much of what I have been saying up to this point. The true believer is "internally motivated" by their "love for God," and this motivation is "supernatural," it doesn't come from the human spirit. This supernatural love, for and from God, produces in the believer the fruit of "reverent worship," "genuine obedience," and a "love for God" and "others" that is not in word only but also in deeds of "self-sacrifice" on their behalf. This is true faith.

In passing, it is significant to make mention that Pastor MacArthur has written an entire book with the title: *Faith Works.* Indeed, it may be said, that a faith that doesn't work is not true faith. George Whitefield, that powerful eighteenth century evangelist, who was so mightily used of God during the Great Awakening in America, had this to say in regards to faith and works, *"A true faith in Jesus Christ . . . fills the heart, so that it cannot be easy till it is doing something for Jesus Christ."* I love this quote as well. If a man, or woman, is truly saved the Spirit of God will produce in them fruitfulness. As believers we are not content being idle spiritually. We long for spiritual fruit. Our hearts desire is to *"lay up treasure in heaven"* (Mark 10:21.)

Salvation, though freely offered, is not without cost. God gave His only begotten Son, and we, because of "*His unspeakable gift,*" will give ourselves back to Him in self-sacrificing service—not to pay Him for our salvation, but out of love and gratitude for having been saved from an eternal hell, and for giving us the amazing privilege of fellowship with Him—here on earth and in heaven forever. If you claim to know Christ but rarely leave your "comfort zone," giving little of your time and effort in *demonstrating* the love to God that you claim to have, then your claim is just so many words. As surely as night follows day, good works follow salvation. Abraham Booth, a prominent English Baptist minister in the late 1700's, said in regards to faith and works:

> "*By obedience to the commands of God, we evidence the sincerity of our holy profession. By this our faith is declared genuine before men . . . Whoever [confesses] to believe in Jesus and is not habitually careful to perform good works, his faith is worthless, barren, dead.*"

This marriage of faith and works is repeated so often in Scripture it would make a long list of verses—following are only a few:

> "*Let your light so shine before men, that they may see your good works and glorify your Father in heaven*" (Matthew 5:16).

> "*That you may have a walk worthy of the Lord, fully pleasing Him, being fruitful in every good work*" (Colossians 1:10).

"*In all things showing yourself to be a pattern of good works*" (Titus 2:9).

"*Remind them . . . to be ready for every good work,*" (Titus 3:1).

"*Affirm constantly that those who have believed in God should be careful to maintain good works*" (Titus 2:7, 3:1, 8).

"*Things that accompany salvation . . . your work and labor of love . . . in that you have ministered to the saints.*" (Hebrews:6:9, 10).

Notice in the last verse in this short list the phrase—"*Things that accompany salvation . . .*" (Hebrews 6:9). The word "*accompany*" is of paramount importance because Scripture is making it clear that our "*work and labor of love*" is an *accompaniment* of salvation. In other words, where there is true salvation, "*good works*" and "*labors of love*" will inevitably be in evidence.

The Apostle Peter in 2 Peter 1:3 makes this marvelous statement, "*As His divine power has given to us all things that pertain to life and godliness, through the knowledge of Him Who called us to glory and virtue.*"

In God's mind and plan for fallen man, our justification "*life*" and our sanctification "*godliness*" always go together. They make one complete package. One does not exist without the other. Lordship salvation antagonists will protest this as departing from grace, but they miss the truth of this verse. All who possess God's "*life*" are justified (born again) and this justification is always accompanied by sanctification ("*godliness,*" holy living.) No one lives a sanctified life who is not *first* justified, and once justified sanctification follows. Sanctification is the *evidence* of justification.

No Lordship advocates present half a gospel, and sadly all too many "decisions" are made on half a gospel, and half a gospel is no gospel! We have no liberty to leave out what God has joined! How many people are in the church who made a "decision" based on half a gospel? How many "came to Christ" for what He could *do* for them, but who never came as sinners, broken and humble at His feet, seeking His mercy, and embracing Him as the Lord and master of their lives? When no real, lasting, ongoing, fruit follows such "conversions" it is evidence, not of true salvation, but of spiritual self-deception.

No one ever received life from God who did not express it outwardly. When the life of God enters the soul of man spiritual barrenness is impossible. "*The Life of God in the Soul of Man,*" is a soul-searching little volume by Puritan, Jeremiah Burroughs, the title of which is an accurate summation of what transpires at conversion. When we are converted "the life of God" enters the "soul of man" and it will not, cannot, be an unfruitful transaction! That would make the Omnipotent God impotent to change the human heart! This is why the Holy Spirit through the Apostle Peter joins "*life and godliness,*" because they cannot exist apart from each other. Anyone claiming to know God (having received His "*life*") who is not outwardly manifesting "*godliness*" through holy living is giving evidence they never did receive the life that God gives.

In the familiar passage on the inspiration of Scripture in 2 Timothy 3:16, 17 the Apostle Paul says, that among the several reasons Scripture is profitable to us, one of them is that, "*the man of God may be thoroughly equipped for every good work.*" This being true, it is accurate then to say that

35

God's Word is working in us to make us fruitful—fruitful in good works. True believers will be continually manifesting the resulting good works that the Word of God, through the Spirit of God, is working in and through them.

The Apostle James also deals very powerfully with this issue of works and true saving faith. In his practical epistle he asks the question, "*What does it profit, my brethren, though a man say he has faith, and has not works; can faith save him?*" (James 2:14). He goes on to answer his own question by giving an imaginary illustration of someone who is cold and hungry coming for help to a professing Christian. In response to this needy person the professing Christian says, "*Depart in peace, be warmed and filled*" (v.16), but doesn't give them anything! James then asks the obvious, "*What does it profit?*" (v.16), and the answer of course is, it profits nothing! James summarizes his argument by saying, "*Even so faith, if it has not works, is dead, being alone*" (v.17). The Apostle James, under the inspiration of the Holy Spirit, is making very clear that the person who *claims* to have faith, but who does not *demonstrate* that claim by their good works, in reality possesses a "*dead*" faith—a faith that cannot save.

Remember who is saying this dear reader! These are not man's words, but God's! The only way anyone can claim to possess genuine faith is to have a faith that actively works! Anything less is a dead faith!

Saved to Serve

In Titus 2:14 we read that God redeemed us in order to have for Himself, "*His own special people, zealous for good works.*" Scripture is telling us here that God saved us to have a "*special*" kind of people, who are "*zealous*" (eager) to do good works. God succeeds in all of His endeavors, so if God saved us to "*have for Himself*" a "*special people*" who would be "*zealous for good works*," then anyone professing faith in Christ who does not have a zeal for good works is possibly not one of God's "*special*" (redeemed) people! (The only possible exception to the above logic is that of a Christian who is living a willfully disobedient life).

From all that you have read up to this point, it is not possible to miss the clear teaching of God's Word concerning faith and works, and yet the church is *full* of people who claim to know God, to be saved, born again, and on their way to heaven, whose lives, for the most part, are lacking in spiritual fruit! To quote again from Charles Haddon Spurgeon:

> "*How sad it is that some talk about their faith in Christ, yet their faith is not proved by their works! . . . A man who is really saved by grace does not need to be told that he is under solemn obligations to serve Christ; the new life within him tells him that. Instead of regarding it as a burden, he gladly surrenders himself—body, soul, and spirit, to the Lord Who has redeemed him, reckoning this to be his reasonable service.*"[8]

Right on Mr. Spurgeon!

So significant, in the mind of God, are our labors of love for Him that the good works we do during our life here on earth have all been *planned* for us in eternity past! Scripture says that, "*We are His workmanship, created in Christ Jesus for good works, which God prepared beforehand that we should walk in them*" (Ephesians 2:10). How significant is that! The English word "*prepared*" ("ordained" in the KJV) is the Greek word *proetoimazo*, which means, "to fit up in advance." This truth is not only an amazing statement of the sovereignty of God but another clear evidence of true salvation. Once again simple logic says that if God, before we were born, has "*prepared*" the good works that we will do for Him here on earth, then anyone claiming to be a Christian who is not engaged in *ongoing* good works is giving testimony to all that he, or she, is not among those who are "*His workmanship*," faithfully living out the "*good works*" which "*God* [has] *prepared beforehand*." Our service for the Lord (our works) proclaim and validate our salvation.

Jesus made it abundantly clear that *every* believer bears fruit. He said for some it will be "*thirtyfold*," for some "*sixtyfold*," and for some a "*hundredfold*," (see Mark 4:20) as was illustrated in the life of Dorcas in Acts 10:36 who was "*full of good works*," but whether it be little fruit or much fruit *all* bear fruit for this is one of the identifying marks of a believer, "*When you bear* (produce) *much fruit, My Father is honored and glorified; and you show and prove yourselves to be true followers of Mine*" (John 15:8, [Amplified version]).

Question: Does your life manifest inward fruit and outward works? Even the most spiritually mature Christian will fall short of God's perfect standard of holy living, nevertheless, can you say in true sincerity that this is the bent and desire of your heart? What good works can you point to? When was the last time you visited someone who was sick, or wrote a letter of encouragement, or made a phone call to specifically minister to someone? How often do you seek to share the gospel? How often do you give out a gospel tract because of your burden for the lost? In what ways are you serving Christ in your church? How much money do you give to God's work? How much time do you spend each day in God's Word and in prayer? If you have to think long and hard about these questions in order to come up with a few good deeds, this is not what the Bible is referring to when it says that God's people are "*zealous*" for good works. For the true believer good works are the normal Christian life, and they flow joyfully and naturally out of a redeemed heart. If these kinds of things are not descriptive of you then you have every reason to ask yourself, "Am I a Christian?

(I wish to include here, in order not to discourage anyone, it is understood that not every believer has the same amount of free time. Retired people, part-time workers, some students, etc., will have more time to devote to the Lord than others who have a more demanding schedule. Most mothers, with children under foot, scarcely have time to eat and sleep, to say nothing of the single parent! Some fathers are in jobs that require after hours work and travel. The Lord knows all this, and He looks on the heart. If changes *can* be made to allow more time we should make them. If we cannot, God knows and understands. Yet, most *everyone* will have at least *some* time to cultivate inward and outward fruit, and if you don't then your priorities are upside down. We all need to make a living, but God expects us to put His Kingdom *first*, and *then* He has promised to meet all our necessary needs—not all our wants. If your job allows you no time at all to serve God and nourish your spiritual life then it's time to look for a different job! If you are too busy to serve God you are too busy.

CHAPTER FOUR

Habitual Sin

The fourth evidence of saving faith is:

4. A true believer does not *live* in *habitual* sin.

> "*Whoever has been born of God does not sin, for His seed remains in him; and he cannot sin, because he has been born of God. In this the children of God and the children of the devil are manifest*" (1 John 3:9, 10).

The importance of the above verse as an evidence of genuine faith cannot be overstated, but before we discuss it further it is necessary to point out that the Apostle is not talking here about being sinless. In 1 John 1:9 we read, "*If we [referring to believers] confess our sins He is faithful and just to forgive us our sins . . .*" This Scripture, and numerous others, plus our own experience teach us that believers can, and do, fall into sin, so when 1 John 3:9,10 is taken in context we see that it is not speaking about sinlessness, but about committing sin *habitually*.

In the verses immediately preceding 1 John 1: 9 and 10 we read: "*Whoever commits sin also commits lawlessness . . .*" "*Little children, let no one deceive you. He who practices righteousness is righteous just as He is righteous. He who sins* (practices is implied) *is of the devil . . .*" (Verses: 3, 7, 8).

These verses provide a crucial test of the new birth. The Apostle John is making it clear that the matter of continuing to sin (habitually *practicing* sin) was how we would know who was and who not was a Christian. But John goes even further and says that a Christian "*cannot sin.*" What does he mean? This statement embodies two marvelous truths:

First, positionally, God sees every believer clothed in the perfect righteousness of Christ. In God's eyes it is wonderfully true that He sees us, in Christ, as sinless, not in living our day to day lives, but in our standing before Him. When we are "*born of God*" God imputes the holy life of Christ to our account, wiping the slate clean of our past, present, *and* future sin. This is a judicious act on God's part in our behalf. When He looks on those who are "*in Christ,*" no matter how imperfect we still are He sees *only* Christ and His righteousness. This is what salvation is—*His* righteousness for *my* unrighteousness! Those who have been placed in Christ through the new birth are "*partakers of the divine nature,*" (2 Peter 1:4) and are holy, spotless, and undefiled in His sight. This is pure grace! It is our only hope of entering heaven—"*Christ in you the hope of glory*" (Colossians 1:27). It is impossible to read of such grace and not shout, Hallelujah!

Because we have then a perfect standing before God in Christ, John is able to say that (in the mind of God) a believer "*cannot sin,*" i.e. commit any sin which God will hold against him and thus exclude him from heaven. Our perfect standing before God is secured by the righteous life and death of Christ and intrinsically (judicially) a believer is unable to sin his or her way out of grace. In the mind of God we are *forever* as righteous as Christ. As a believer this ought to cause you to fall on your knees in adoring, thankful praise, and wonder that He would choose you as one of His own.

There are those who argue that the eternal security and righteous standing of the believer encourages loose living since all our sins, past, present, and even future are all paid for and forgiven, and we can do nothing to lose our salvation. Such reasoning is spurious and belies a seriously faulty doctrinal understanding of grace. Instead of causing the believer to live loosely, or to sin easily, the exact opposite is true. When we as believers comprehend what God has done for us in Christ our hearts are filled with such amazement and wonder for such undeserved kindness that we only want to serve Him *more.*

Secondly, and in context, the primary meaning of what the Apostle is referring to when he says a Christian "*cannot sin,*" is that while experientially (in every day life) Christians can and do sin, no true believer can live in a *habitual* pattern of sin. In other words no one who is born again can go on living in the same old habit patterns of sin after conversion as before conversion. The "*seed,*" spoken of in verse nine as remaining in the believer, is referring to the life of God—that eternal holy life which, in the person of the Holy Spirit, takes up permanent residence in every born again child of God. It is the indwelling Holy Spirit who is the One who *restrains* the believer from living in unbroken sin. The true Christian "*cannot sin*" habitually because in Christ he has died to sin, not just judicially but actually. A miracle of God transpires in every convert's heart that puts an end to habitual sin patterns. The Apostle Paul explains it this way, "*How shall we who died to sin live any longer in it?*" (Romans 6:2). The implied answer to this question is we *cannot* live any longer in it! It is not possible for a true believer in Christ to live in unbroken patterns of sin as they once did. If they are so living, they make God out to be a liar, and give testimony to all around them that they are *not* truly saved, and do *not* possess His holy "*seed*" within.

It is our natural tendency, due to our fallen nature, to justify and defend ourselves, to seek to put the best construction on our sins and failures. This is not only sinful in itself but has a built in judgment attached, "*He who covers his sins will not prosper, but whoever confesses and forsakes them will have mercy* (Proverbs 28:13).

When reading in Scripture that a Christian cannot habitually live in sin our natural tendency is to think of the grosser sins, such as murder, stealing, lying, fornication, adultery, drunkenness, etc., and say to ourselves that since I do not live that way I must be doing okay. In thinking this way we conveniently forget that in God's eyes *all* sin is heinous and worthy of His judgment. Never forget that "the little white lie" you told nailed Him to the cross as much as the murderers knife. "*For whoever shall keep the whole law, and yet stumble in one point he is guilty of all*" (James 2:10). The same law that commands us not to kill also commands us to, "*love your neighbor.*" Being unkind and unloving are sins deserving of hell no less than murder and adultery are. In taking stock of our lives, and in making a genuine assessment of our true spiritual condition, we must not allow Satan, or our fallen hearts, to blind our eyes to what "habitual" sinning actually is. To live in habitual sin has to do with the *whole* of God's law. The point I am trying to make is this—to live in habitual sin encompasses *all* the precepts and commands of God, not simply what men consider the grosser sins. Therefore, if we are *habitually* unkind then we are habitually sinning just the same as someone who habitually lives an immoral life or who habitually lies and steals. True believers do not habitually violate *any* of God's precepts and commands; they *cannot* live this way and legitimately profess to be believers.

If the Holy Spirit is resident within us He will sensitize our conscience, but we must humbly submit our lives to His Lordship and control. Receiving Gods new life at conversion does not mean we are instantly perfected, but it does mean we now hate what we once loved, and instead of enjoying sin we are grieved over it, and we long to grow in grace and holiness.

If you are a true believer you will not consider any sin insignificant. If the Holy Spirit has put His searchlight on your life as you have been reading this book, and you have been excusing yourself in any way, then it may be a warning sign that you are not a true believer. Instead of excusing ourselves, the attitude of a true believer is expressed by Job, and every saint of God in both the Old and New Testaments, when he came face to face with God's holiness and his own corruption: "*I have heard of You by the hearing of the ear, but now my eye sees You. Therefore I abhor myself, and repent in dust and ashes*" (Job 42:5, 6). To be exposed to the holiness of God on the pages of Scripture is to, like Job, "*abhor*" ourselves. When the Holy Spirit puts His finger on our lives true believers repent and obey, unbelievers excuse themselves and continue on in self-deception.

What are we to say, in conclusion, about men and women within the church who claim to be saved but are living together? Well, the Word of God is either true when it says that a Christian "*cannot*" live in habitual sin, or it is not true. Since God "*cannot lie,*" the only conclusion we are left with is that those who habitually sin are *not* Christians!

What is God's *standard* for those who profess His name? "*Only let your [conduct] be worthy of the gospel . . . that you may be blameless and innocent, children of God without blemish in the midst of a crooked and perverse generation, among whom you shine as lights in the world*" (Philippians 1:27, 2:15, ESV

Scripture is clear—a habitually sinning lifestyle is *not* possible for a believer. If you are living this way then you are deceiving yourself that you are a Christian—regardless if you can point to a conversion experience. You may have gone through a "religious" experience when you "received" Christ, but your heart was not changed.

A final clarifying point is in order before moving on to the next chapter:

An occasional stumble in a moment of weakness is not in view in this chapter. We all struggle with our sin natures and will struggle until we are freed from this "*body of death.*" It is not only possible for believers, but likely, that we will occasionally give into temptation and fall into sin, even gross sin, but to *continue* living habitually in a pattern of sin is simply not possible for true believers.

CHAPTER FIVE

God's Discipline

The fifth evidence of saving faith is:

5. A true believer will *experience* God's *discipline* when they sin.

> "*For whom the Lord loves He chastens, and scourges every son whom He receives*" (Hebrews 12:6).

This fifth evidence of salvation is closely connected to the fourth. Unbelievers, by default, live the whole of their lives in habitual sinning patterns, but God's children cannot persist in patterns of sinning without God's intervention through discipline. Human parents only discipline the children that belong to them, not someone else's. The family of God is no different. God will punish the wicked, but discipline is reserved for His own.

God's discipline is a sign of sonship and comes in two forms, public and private. If sins committed are public then the church is commanded by God to discipline its sinning members, first, in private, with the individual alone, and finally in the corporate assembly if necessary. See Matthew 18:15-17, 2 Corinthians 12:14-13:3, 2 Thessalonians 3:14, 15, 1 Corinthians 5:9-13. If the sin committed is private (unknown to others) God has promised to discipline His sinning child if they do not confess and forsake their sin. And this promised discipline is a clear scriptural evidence of true conversion.

In regards to publically committed sins, in spite of the teaching of Scripture, the instruction for church discipline is largely ignored in evangelical churches. This is a serious sin of omission and a sad commentary on the state of the Evangelical Church. What the church has chosen to ignore, or consider relatively unimportant, is in reality a cancer, that, like leaven, "*leavens the whole lump*" (1 Corinthians 5:6.) Sin tolerated within the body of Christ will dull the effectiveness of our witness, and will work like dry rot in undermining sound doctrine.

If the church will not obey God in this matter she will give an account for it on the day that we stand before Him. He will not be mocked, and He is not bound by our faithlessness. "*If we are faithless, He remains faithful*" (2 Timothy 2:13.)

As was discussed in the fourth evidence of saving faith, it is not uncommon today to hear something like the following concerning someone who claims to be a Christian, "But I know so and so who is a Christian and he has been living with his girlfriend for years!" What are we to say to this, or to *any* kind of *habitual* sin? There are two things that need to be said regarding habitual sin and someone claiming to have faith in Christ:

First, we know from Scripture, and as we have already pointed out, believers can, and do, fall into sin, and every true believer who does, and who refuses to acknowledge their sin and repent, and turn from it, will, according to Scripture, come under God's discipline. The defining verses on this truth are found in Hebrews 12:5-8. In verses 5 and

6 the writer of Hebrews quotes from Proverbs 3:11, 12, *"My Son do not despise the chastening of the Lord, nor be discouraged when you are rebuked by Him; for whom the Lord loves He chastens, and scourges every son whom He receives."*

The second thing that needs to be said regarding this is found in verse 8 of Hebrews 5, *"But if you are without chastening, of which all have become partakers, then you are illegitimate and not sons."* It is clear from this scripture that *"all"* of God's children experience discipline when they continue in the practice of sin, and any who are *"without"* God's discipline are *"illegitimate"* children. In other words, a true child of God cannot get away with sinning, and if they *are* getting away with it (i.e. continuing to sin without experiencing God's discipline) then God says they are *not* His children! Strong words that all who profess faith in Christ need to take very seriously!

I think it is important to say, lest we discourage or mislead any genuine believer who may be struggling with a particular sinful habit or weakness, that though a true believer *can* fall into sin, true believers cannot *remain* in sin without anguish of heart. True believers will be grieved over their sin, and no true believer can know peace of heart while living in sin. This grief, produced by the indwelling Spirit, is in itself a *evidence* of salvation. If you, as a believer, are experiencing repeated failure in an area, or areas of your life, but you hate it and long to be free from it, take heart. Unbelievers do not long for holiness of life. If there is a genuine relationship between God and us there will be genuine sorrow and grief over anything that separates our spirit from His. If God is our true Father, then we, His true children, who possess His holy nature, will hate sin, and when we do sin we will despise it in ourselves and grieve over it. This grief, as I said, is an evidence of salvation. Unbelievers may feel guilt and remorse, but not Spirit produced grief.

If you despise the sin that separates you from God and experience grieving produced by the Holy Spirit, this marks you as one of God's own dear children, and rather than be discouraged or doubt your salvation, rejoice that God is dealing with you, and then *repent* and *stop* sinning!

Let me emphasize one more time, it is equally true, that if you can continue to practice habitual sin without Spirit produced grief, or the discipline of God, (all the while feeling confident you are a Christian) it is a huge red flag that you are sadly deceived.

How God Disciplines

In what ways does God discipline His children? It will always first be by a convicting conscience which is immediate and persistent in a true believer. If conscience is ignored God is not impotent in bringing about the desired repentance—be it sickness, financial loss, trials, various misfortunes, and ultimately even death. God is very longsuffering, and no one knows how long He will patiently deal with His rebellious child before He takes more serious steps, but one thing is certain from scripture—no true believer can continue to go on living in habitual, known, sin *without* experiencing God's discipline.

If we choose to ignore the Holy Spirit's first built in warning mechanism, that of conscience, we will eventually dull its convicting power. This is extremely serious and will, have a devastating effect on your spiritual health. If we allow ourselves to become insensitive to our conscience it will only make it easier for us to sin. If what once convicted you doesn't bother you very much anymore, take heed, you are playing a very dangerous game with God that will only have serious consequences if persisted in! If you have been ignoring the voice of conscience you need to immediately repent of your rebellion against the Holy Spirit, and plead with God to cleanse your heart and, "*restore a right spirit within [you]*" (Psalm 51:10), as King David did when he stopped ignoring his conscience and faced up to his sin with Bathsheba.

God's dealings with King David provide us with valuable insights into the function of conscience in a believer. This is graphically illustrated in Psalm 32:3, 4. In this psalm David describes his inward struggle when he stubbornly refused to acknowledge his sin, "*When I kept silent, my bones grew old through my groaning all the day long. For day and night your hand was heavy upon me; my vitality was turned into the drought of summer.*" True believers will experience, as did David, an inward "*groaning*", "*heaviness*" of heart, and lack of "*vitality*" when they refuse to acknowledge their sin. An accusing conscience is nothing less then the disciplining hand of God in our lives and we ought to rejoice in it for it is one of the *evidences* that we are in His family—receiving a Father's correction. No child of God lacks the convicting work of the Spirit, "*The spirit of a man is the lamp of the Lord, searching all the inner depths of his heart*" (Proverbs 20:27).

The late Adrian Rogers, pastor and popular radio speaker on the program *Love Worth Finding*, had this to say in a radio message concerning sin and heart conviction: "*If you can sin and forget about it you are not saved.*" A simple and straightforward statement, typical of the godly wisdom of Adrian Rogers, but oh how true! The difference between a true believer and someone with false assurance will be this inner, subjective, experience of true sorrow and grief over sins committed. An unbeliever may feel remorse, even deep remorse, but because they do not possess the indwelling Spirit they are able to quell their conscience, forget it, and *continue* in their sinful patterns of living. If you find this is generally descriptive of your experience, then, my dear friend, you are deceived about your salvation.

But what about the Christian who *is* truly saved and yet *does* persists in sin? It is possible for a believer to continue in a pattern of sin for a time. God is longsuffering, but His patience does have an end. The Bible teaches that a Christian who stubbornly refuses to repent may eventually be judged by death (cf. I John 5:16 and I Corinthians 5:5). This, of course, is God's *ultimate* discipline, and it is tragic. God alone knows when the time arrives for this final step. Again, we are playing a dangerous and deadly game with God when we choose to ignore God's gracious provision of conscience. I have personally, in the early years of my Christian life, witnessed this tragedy play out in the life of a brother who was involved sexually with a girl in the church. She became pregnant, and when confronted with his sin and his responsibility to the girl, he remained unrepentant, refusing the working of God's Spirit in his life, and even though he was very young, he developed cancer, and God took him home within a very short time. This left an indelible impression on my life.

It is important to say also that just because a Christian is going through some of the above-mentioned trials, such as sickness, financial loss, misfortune, etc., it does not in any way, *necessarily*, imply that God is disciplining them. Trials and sufferings are the human lot, and God uses suffering in *all* of our lives to conform us into the likeness of His Son. Only God, and the person undergoing the trial, know whether the cause of their suffering is due to unconfessed sin. If it becomes known, publically, that a brother or sister in the body is involved in sin, then the church is instructed in Matthew 18 to exercise church discipline, and we "*who are spiritual*" (Galatians 6:1) are to help in restoring them, but we must *never* assume that God is judging a brother or sister simply because they are experiencing trials. In Scripture God's choicest saints, e.g. Job, Joseph, Daniel, Esther, and the Apostles, to name just a few, have undergone the severest of trials which were not due to any unconfessed sin.

To tie together and summarize evidences four and five, we see the following truths:

1. A true Christian *cannot* live in a *continuous, habitual,* state of sinning (I John 3:9).
2. If a true believer commits sin they will be *grieved* over their sin, (if they haven't dulled their conscience) and will find no rest of heart until they confess their sin and forsake it (Psalm 51).
3. If a true believer continues to sin they *will* experience God's discipline. And the grieving, as well as the discipline, are both *evidences* of salvation (Hebrews 12:5-8). (This evidence is referring only to *personal* and *private* discipline by the Lord. When public church discipline is exercised it does not imply the sinning person is a true believer).
4. If a true Christian continues to sin and refuses to repent and turn from their sin the word of God teaches that such disobedience could ultimately lead to an untimely death (1 John5:16, 1 Corinthians 5:5).
5. If someone claiming to know Christ continues to commit sin, day after day, month after month,

year after year, and God does not intervene with discipline, then Scripture plainly teaches that such a person is *not* a true child of God, but is illegitimate and thus deceived about their salvation. (Hebrews 5:8, I John 2:3, 4).

Question: What is your experience when you sin? Do you identify with David's struggles in Psalm 32? Is your spirit immediately grieved? Does your conscience trouble you? Do you lose the peace you once possessed? Are you aware of broken fellowship between yourself and God? Do you find yourself avoiding Bible reading and prayer? Is church attendance, and being around God's people, something you no longer enjoy as you once did? If you persist in sinning does God intervene in your life through discipline? If you are a true believer and have ever fallen into sin, and persisted in it for a time you will be able to identify with the above experiences. If the above are not descriptive of your experience you need to reexamine your professed salvation.

Chapter Six

Longing for His Coming

The sixth and final evidence of saving faith is:

6.   A true believer expectantly *looks for the second coming* of Christ.

> "*For our citizenship is in heaven, from which we also eagerly wait for the Savior, the Lord Jesus Christ*" (Philippians 3:20).

Every true child of God "*eagerly waits,*" i.e. looks forward to, with expectancy and longing, the return of Christ. Randy Alcorn, in his wonderful little book on heaven, *In Light of Eternity*, (subtitled: *Perspectives on Heaven*,) had this to say about a believer's attitude toward heaven:

> "*The more we understand this world is not our home and the more we lay up our treasures in heaven, the more we will long for heaven and the more content we'll be to leave earth behind. God doesn't expect us to long for death—He does expect us to long for heaven.*"

The children of God are not at home in this world and our thoughts often are of our heavenly home. The longer we live the more does the hope of heaven characterize our lives, or ought to. As we grow older and our vital life forces recede the less enamored we are with the things of earth, and we "*groan within ourselves*" (Romans 8:23) having learned by experience that this earth cannot satisfy our hearts. The words of King David express the longing of all the redeemed, "*I shall be satisfied when I awake with Thy likeness*" (Psalm 17:15). There is no real satisfaction until that glorious day. The Apostle Paul, in like manner, as representative of all New Testament saints, knew the same heart longing as David, "*I am hard pressed . . . having a desire to depart and be with Christ, which is far better*" (Philippians 1:23). Paul was torn between two worlds as all believers are.

This book began with the first and greatest evidence of salvation, which is the evidence of love—love for God and love for our fellow man. This love, given to us by the Holy Spirit at conversion, motivates the heart of a true believer towards heavenly mindedness. A common cliché that is sometimes quoted concerning some Christians is that, "He, or she, is so heavenly minded they are no earthly good!" This should never be true of a believer! The Apostle John said of our hope of heaven in 1 John 3:3 that, "*Everyone who has this hope in Him purifies himself, just as He is pure.*" The more heavenly minded a Christian becomes the more earthly good he or she *should* be! We are saved to serve God and others, not to be idle, and our longing for heaven ought to make us better fathers and mothers, better husbands and wives, better parents, better employees and employers, better citizens, etc. Our heavenly home that awaits us is not a "pie in the sky" pipe dream, but reality, ultimate reality, and should make a very real difference in how we live our lives day to day in this world.

To say you love God but a longing for heaven is not part of your Christian experience is to call in question your profession. When you met your wife and eventually fell in love with her you found you could not get enough of her presence—right? In fact, that is perhaps the number one reason people get married—they want to be *with* the person they love 24/7! This is only normal. It would be strange indeed when you were courting your wife if you didn't anticipate, with delight, the times you would be with her. If you didn't plan for and look forward to those times no matter how much you told her you loved her your lack of enthusiasm would speak louder than your words. No doubt she would begin to question whether you *really* did love her. It is no different when one is captured by the love of Christ. No earthly lover can compare with the desirability of the person of Christ. The more one gets to know Him the more one longs to know Him, and just as an earthly lover has reason to doubt the affections of the one loved who placed no priority on being with them, so those who profess love to Christ but have little longing to be with Him in heaven, or who, here on earth, place no priority on times of communion with Him in personal, private, fellowship, or in faithful public worship, are not fooling God, "*who searches the hearts*" (Romans 8:27).

This desire and longing for heaven is not just *thinking* about heaven. In reality, it is not primarily conscious thoughts of heaven that we are speaking of in this sixth evidence of salvation. Pondering (thinking of) the wonders and glory to come is certainly a very real part of "*eagerly waiting for the Savior,*" but the longing we are speaking of goes much deeper even than our conscious thought life and arises as naturally as breathing out of our re-created spirit. We don't think about breathing it is just something that is *always* there. We do not *always* consciously think of heaven, but the longing for it is *always* there. This is so because as believers we are "*one spirit*" with the Lord,"—"*he who is joined to the Lord is one spirit with Him*" (1 Corinthians 6:17)—and our true identity, our true home, is found where He is. We are "*sojourners and pilgrims*" (1 Peter 2:11) in this sinful world, and having, "*tasted that that the Lord is gracious*" (1 Peter 2:3) we know the best is still future. Earthly comforts and material possessions simply cannot provide the fulfillment we long for, and were created for. For us, the wells of earth are all "*broken cisterns,*" (Jeremiah 2:13) only, "*In His presence is fullness of joy,*" only, "*At His right hand are pleasures forevermore*" (Psalm 16:11). In His high priestly prayer, Jesus prayed, "*Father, I desire that they also, whom You have given Me, may be with Me where I am*" (John 17:24, ESV). What a humbling realization this is! *We* long to be with Him, and, wonder of wonders, *He* longs to be with us!

Mere professors of faith in Christ are simply not able to enter into these kinds of holy longings, which resonate in the heart of true believers. While they may profess to believe in heaven, they reveal what their true heart affections are by spending nearly all of their time and energy on the things of this world. But for the believer it is different, "*While we do not look at the things which are seen, but at the things which are not seen. For the things which are seen are temporary, but the things which are not seen are eternal*" (2 Corinthians 4:18).

If you are a believer but the anticipation of heaven is not an on-going reality in your heart then you need to ask yourself whether you have "*left your first love*" (Revelation 2:4), and have become enamored with this present world system, as did certain believers in the Ephesian church to whom Christ spoke the above sad words. If this is true of you, then *listen* and *respond* to what our Lord had further to say to them, and to His Church today as well, "*Remember therefore from where you have fallen; repent and do the first works*" (Revelation 2:5). "*Remember.*" "*Repent.*" "*Do.*" In other words believer, recall to mind ("*remember*") your coldness of heart, ask for forgiveness ("*repent*") for leaving your first love, and return ("*do the first works*") to the fervency of the faith and love you once had for Christ.

Question: Is the hope of Christ's return a *constant* source of joy in your life? Do you long to see Him? Do the things of this world mean little to you when compared to the eternal treasures that await you? Do you hold your earthly possessions loosely knowing that "*in a moment, in the twinkling of an eye,*" (I Corinthians 15:52) you will leave them all behind for the real and lasting riches, or is your heart and your desires firmly fixed on the things of this world? Does this longing to see Christ, as the Apostle Peter says, fill you with "*joy unspeakable, and full of glory?*" (1 Peter 1:8). These experiences, and emotions, in relation to heaven, do not describe the unredeemed.

As we conclude this sixth, and last, evidence of genuine conversion the following might seem blunt but it is spoken in sincere love and with the earnest prayer that God, through His Holy Spirit, may jar awake any who may be deceived about their eternal destiny:

> "*If the thought of heaven is not a constant, joyous, realization in your experience, if you have little desire and longing for the life to come it may be an indication that the life to come, for you, may not be heaven!*"

Concluding Sobering Thoughts

It is said that, "The path to hell is paved by good intentions." How tragically true this is! There are countless individuals, many of whom are very sincere and good intentioned, who are sadly deceived about their own eternal destiny. Perhaps you are among that group as you read these words. I beg you, in the name of Jesus Christ and for the sake of your eternal soul, to continue to read the following with an open and transparent heart.

There will be no more shocking and tragic scene on judgment day than that spoken of by our Lord in Matthew 7:23 when those who have claimed to be His followers, who thought they were on their way to heaven, will hear Christ say to them, "*I never knew you; depart from me.*" Countless numbers on that day will find the gates of heaven shut to them! This tragedy of all tragedies need never happen to you. If your ears someday ever hear those unthinkable words out of the mouth of Jesus Christ, the blame will not be His, for God has plainly revealed to us in His word *what* genuine faith is, and how we can be *sure* we possess it. Let me say also, with deep sorrow of heart, the very fact that you hold this book in your hands will make your judgment on that day more severe if you fail to heed its warning.

What has been dealt with in this book has not been the opinion of a man. Every evidence of salvation presented herein is taken from Scripture. With prayer and tears over the plight of those who are deceived I have poured out my heart concerning God's own heart. Jesus divided all of humanity with the following words, "*Everyone who is of the truth hears My voice*" (John 18:3). Have you heard His voice as you have read this book? Has it brought joy to you, or has it disturbed your mind and brought nagging doubts? Do not let the enemy of your soul deceive you into thinking all is well if it is not.

We have examined six evidences of genuine conversion, which in varying degrees will be the experience of every true child of God. These evidences are not given to intimidate anyone who is truly saved into doubting their salvation. No one but Jesus Christ was able to say, "*I always do those things that please Him*" (John 8:29). Perfection is not attainable in this life, we all fail, yet we can all take heart and rejoice as we see, even through our failures, these six evidences of salvation manifested, in some measure, in our own hearts and lives.

In summary, the six evidences of true conversion that we have looked at are:

1. A true believer *possesses* God's *love* in their heart.
2. A true believer *lives* an *obedient* life.
3. A true believer is a *fruit bearing* Christian.
4. A true believer *cannot* live in *habitual* sin.
5. A true believer *experiences* God's *discipline* when they sin.
6. A true believer *looks* for the *Second Coming* of Christ.

CHAPTER SEVEN

Making Sure

The following summary statement embodies the whole purpose of this book:

> *If the evidences of salvation, set forth in this book, are present in your life then you can rejoice in the Lord with a grateful heart that you are among the elect of God. If the evidences of salvation set forth in this book are not present then your greatest need is to prostrate yourself before God, pleading with Him to be gracious to you and to open your eyes to see your true spiritual condition, and to ask that He would grant you repentance, and genuine saving faith.*

If in reading to this last chapter you have become convicted in your heart that your life does not consistently reflect the scriptural evidences of true conversion then this chapter is by far the most important chapter for you because making sure of heaven is the most important thing in life. This is the one thing in life, above all others, we *must* be certain about. "Hope so's" won't do. The possibility of deception is very real. Don't allow a head knowledge of Christ to keep you from a heart knowledge of Him. One saves, the other damns.

Perhaps you have been thinking to yourself, "Who can live like this; this is for the super-spiritual, not for common folks?" If this is how you are thinking then you have gotten the point! You *cannot* live like this; I can't, you can't; no one can! This is *super-natural* living! Only the new birth can supply the power for such a life. For the natural man, even for the "religious" man, it is an impossible life, "*But the natural man does not receive the things of the Spirit of God, for they are foolishness to him; nor can he know them, because they are spiritually discerned* (understood)" (1 Corinthians 2:14). But for the redeemed, who possess *God's* Holy Spirit living within them, it is the "abundant life" Christ promised.

If the Holy Spirit has used this book to arouse even the slightest doubt in your mind as to whether or not you are truly converted, then, for the sake of your eternal soul, I ask you to examine your heart before God. Not later, not tomorrow, but now. "*Behold, now is the accepted time; behold, now is the day of salvation.*" (2 Corinthians 6:2). Do not entertain the lies of the evil one and begin to make excuses. His lies are quite familiar—they go something like this:

"Oh, I am all right."
"I am not a bad or evil person."
"Nobody is perfect."
"God knows I am doing the best I can."
"God is too good and too loving to send me to hell."
"I believe in Jesus."

Satan will do his utmost to side track the masses from the real issues of life, and to take our minds off the clear gospel message.

No, you are not "all right" if these six evidences are not *clearly* seen in your life.

No, as unkind as it might sound, you *are* an "evil person" if you are not converted. You may be "religious" and "good" in the eyes of men, but it was Jesus Who said to the most "religious" people of His day, "*you are of your father the devil*" (John 8:44). Why did Jesus say something as seemingly unkind and unloving as that? It was because they were seeking to come to God on their own terms. They were embracing Satan's religion and were blind to the danger they were in. In reality Jesus' statement was a loving statement. If they would stop their hypocritical pretending and look into their hearts and heed Christ's warning it was meant to lead them from an eternal hell to eternal heaven. There is no neutral ground, either you belong to God by coming to Him *on His terms* or you belong to Satan. There are only two kinds of people in the world: children of God or children of the evil one.

Yes, it is true that "no one is perfect," but God *demands* perfection if we hope to spend eternity with Him. This is why we "*must be born again*" for only then does Christ's righteousness (His perfection) become ours. Only then do the doors of heaven swing open to us, and we become (in God's eyes, through grace) as righteous as His Son, and "*joint-heirs*" with Christ (Romans 8:17).

Scripture is unmistakably clear, it is not "doing the best we can" for "*all have sinned and fall short of the glory of God*" (Romans 3:23) Our best efforts are "*filthy rags*" in His sight (Isaiah 64:5).

Yes, God is "good and loving," but He is also holy and just and *must* punish sin—unless we have accepted His plan of redemption through the substitutionary death of Christ. For God to overlook your sin would bring Him down to your level, and be tantamount to making Him an unjust judge. Sin has consequences, here on earth, and eternally. God is a holy and righteous judge, and a righteous judge must meet out a just penalty for every transgression of the law. God cannot welcome unpunished sin into heaven where all are holy. That is what the "Good News" of the gospel is all about! God *did* punish your sins when he laid them on Christ Who bore God's wrath in your place. The Bible says that, "*God is not willing that any should perish*" (2 Peter 3:9). The only people who go to hell are those who *choose* to go there (against God's desire and willingness to save them) by refusing His offer of forgiveness through Christ, and instead seek acceptance with God on their own terms.

Last, "believing" in the death and resurrection of Christ on your behalf does not save if it has never made the trip from your head to your heart. Remember that Satan and all his demons have accurate head knowledge of all the facts about Christ but they are eternally lost! Head knowledge equals information. Heart knowledge (the transfer of head knowledge into sincere commitment) equals salvation.

To face death without Jesus Christ means eternal existence in hell. This a tragedy too enormous to put into words. If it were possible to spend one microsecond in hell it would be sufficient to cause any rational mind to "*flee from the wrath to come*," (Luke 3:7) but one microsecond there will be one microsecond too late, for Jesus made it clear that, "*it is appointed for men to die once but after this the judgment*" (Hebrews 9:27). (Also Luke 16:19-31) There is no second chance, no Purgatory. Death ends all opportunities to repent. Once a soul enters hell their presence there is sealed forever. Tragically, according to the

Word of God, most of humanity will not flee His wrath, but instead choose hell (intentionally or unintentionally) rather than submit their lives to Christ. I again beg of you not to make this tragic mistake.

If you have honestly answered the many searching questions in this book, and you know that your life is lacking the consistent, clear, evidences of genuine conversion, then God's mercy and grace are being extended to you in this very moment.

All that God requires of you is that you come to Him in true repentance, acknowledging your sinful condition, and recognizing that there is nothing you can do to become acceptable to Him. God Himself has provided the full payment for all your sin, placing the punishment you deserve on His own Son—"*Who gave Himself a ransom for all*" (1 Timothy 2:6). After His crucifixion He was buried, and three days later He rose from the dead in triumph over death, sin, the devil and hell, and has become, "*the author of eternal salvation to all who obey Him*" (Hebrews 5:9).

A word of warning is important here. It is at this critical juncture in the conversion experience that Satan desires to work his deception in order to lure as many as he can into a false commitment. It is so very crucial to make crystal clear that "saying a prayer," in itself, does not save anyone. God is only looking at our hearts, and if you are tired of going your own way, and are truly repentant, ready to forsake your sin and to make Christ the Lord of your life, then a sincere prayer of repentance is always heard. He has promised, "*He that comes to Me I will by no means cast out*" (John 6:37).

If you understand all this, and desire to come to Christ, you can pray to Him right now in your own words, or you can pray the following prayer, making it the sincere expression of your heart:

"Dear God, I know that I am a sinner. I confess that I have often broken Your holy laws, and justly deserve Your punishment. I acknowledge that all my own attempts to live a godly life have fallen miserably short of Your perfect standard. I repent this day of my sin, and I turn from it. I believe that Jesus Christ died in my place, taking upon Himself the punishment for all my sin and I now receive Him into my heart and life as my Savior and as the Lord of my life. I surrender myself wholly to You, and I desire, with Your help, to follow and serve You all the rest of my days. I pray this in Jesus' name. Amen."

If you have prayed this prayer sincerely, God Who is faithful to His Word, has promised to forgive your sin, *"For whoever calls upon the name of the Lord shall be saved"* (Romans 10:13).

Once you become a believer you pass from a state of spiritual death to spiritual life and become a member of God's family. It is the start of a whole new life and the following things are absolutely vital and necessary for your spiritual growth:

1. Talk to God, *daily*, in prayer, and let Him talk to you through His word—the Bible.
2. Find a Bible believing Church, where the *whole* Bible is taught—a church where the pastor is a qualified and committed, verse by verse, *expositor* of the Scriptures, who through sound theological training, and diligent study, has earned the right to be heard.

3. Be a witnessing Christian, telling others how they too can find eternal life in Christ.
4. Tell someone (another believer) about the decision you have just made.

Knowing Jesus Christ is life's greatest adventure! Intimate fellowship with Him brings a joy that nothing else in life can even be compared to. The Westminster Catechism correctly states that: "The chief end of man is to glorify God and enjoy Him forever." While we look forward to the joy of heaven, the joys of heaven begin here on earth. The amount of our joy is in direct proportion to how much we seek to "glorify God." God is no man's debtor. "*If anyone loves Me, he will keep My word, and My Father will love him, and We will come to him and make our home with him*" (John 14:23.)

If you have come to faith in Jesus Christ for the first time as a result of reading this book the author would ask that you share this with him. Likewise, if by reading this book the Holy Spirit has brought you to an assurance of salvation that you didn't have before please share this with the author.

(The author can be contacted at <u>richardbarton37@gmail.com</u>)

NOTES

Introduction

[1]   Arthur Pink, *Practical Christianity* (Grand Rapids, Mich.: Baker Publishing Group, © 1974), p.20

[2]   Tozer, *Man: The Dwelling Place of God*, (Wingspread Publishers © 1966) p.30-33.

[3]   J.C. Ryle, *Holiness* (Reprint, Durham, England: Evangelical Press, ©1979), p.29-30

Chapter One

[4]   Thomas Boston, *Human Nature In It's Fourfold State*, (London: The Banner of Truth Trust) p.209

[5]   John Piper, *God's Passion for His Glory*, (Crossway Books) p.111

[6]   Charles Haddon Spurgeon, *Being God's Friends*, (Used by permission of Whitaker House © 1997) p.102 (www. whitakerhouse.com).

Chapter Two

[7]   John MacArthur, *MacArthur Study Bible*, (Word Publishing) © 1997, p. 1797

[8]   C.H. Spurgeon, *The Metropolitan Tabernacle Pulpit*, vol. 56 (reprint, Pasadena, Tex.: Pilgrim, © 1979), 617

Chapter Six

9   Randy Alcorn, Reprinted from, *In Light of Eternity.*
Copyright © 1999 by Eternal Perspectives Ministries. (Used
by permission of WaterBrook Press, Colorado Springs, CO)
All rights reserved; p.160